P9-EDO-334

MAKING CONNECTIONS 1:

An Integrated Approach to Learning English

MAKING CONNECTIONS 1:

An Integrated Approach to Learning English

Carolyn Kessler

Linda Lee

Mary Lou McCloskey

Mary Ellen Quinn

Lydia Stack

Heinle & Heinle Publishers
An International Thomson Publishing Company
Boston, MA 02116, U.S.A.

I(T)P

The publication of *Making Connections* was directed by the members of the Heinle & Heinle Secondary ESL Publishing Team:

Editorial Director:	Roseanne Mendoza
Senior Production Services Coordinator:	Lisa McLaughlin
Market Development Director:	Ingrid Greenberg
Developmental Editor:	Nancy Jordan

Also Participating in the publication of this program were:

Publisher:	Stan Galek
Director of Production:	Elizabeth Holthaus
Senior Assistant Editor:	Sally Conover
Manufacturing Coordinator:	Mary Beth Hennebury
Composition:	GTS Graphics
Project Management:	GTS Graphics
Interior Design:	Martucci Studio
Illustration:	Jerry Malone/Martucci Studio
Cover Design:	Martucci Studio

Manufactured in the United States of America

ISBN: *Making Connections 1* 0-8384-7008-4

Heinle & Heinle Publishers is an International Thomson Publishing Company

10 9 8 7 6 5 4 3 2

PREFACE

Middle and High School ESOL (English for Speakers of Other Languages) students are faced with a formidable task. In the few short years of school that remain, they must learn both English and the challenging content of their academic curriculum, made more challenging because so much language acquisition is demanded. *Making Connections: An Integrated Approach to Learning English* provides resources to integrate the teaching and learning of language and academic content. These resources help teachers and students develop students' ability to communicate in English as they focus on motivating themes with topics, activities, tools, and procedures that introduce the content areas of science, social studies, and literature.

Making Connections: An Integrated Approach to Learning English is designed to help secondary students and their teachers reach toward important, essential goals and to facilitate their learning language and content in the ways they learn best. What are the goals we reach for?

Joy—the joy in life and learning that will make our students happy, successful lifetime learners

Literacy—the ability to use reading and writing to accomplish amazing things

Community—the knowledge that they live in an accepting community where they have rights, responsibilities, and resources

Access—access to whatever resources they need to accomplish their own goals, including access to technology

Power—the power to make their lives into whatever they choose

What are the ways of teaching and learning that work best, according to our understanding of language acquisition research? The answer, we believe, is through **integrated learning**. *Making Connections* includes four different kinds of integration: language areas, language and academic content, students with one another, and school with the larger community.

- We integrate language areas through active learning.

We combine reading, writing, listening, and speaking into things that students **do**. Through interaction with authentic and culturally relevant literature, through activities that involve genuine communication, and through student-owned process writing, students learn the "parts" or "skills" of language in meaningful "whole" contexts.

- We integrate language with academic content and processes.

Language is best learned when it is used as a tool, when students are meaningfully engaged in something important to them. Learning the language and participating in processes specific to the academic content area subjects are essential for preparing students to move into mainstream content-area classrooms. By teaching language through content, we attempt to do several things at once: we help students to learn to use a variety of learning strategies; introduce them to science, social studies and literature content appropriate for their age and grade levels; and help them to use accessible language and learn new essential language in the process.

- We integrate students with one another.

We help teachers and students develop a real learning community in which students and teacher use a variety of strategies—including many cooperative learning strategies—to accomplish student-owned educational goals. We acknowledge that students are not all at the same level linguistically or academically but recognize that each student has strengths to offer in your classroom, so we provide choices of materials and activities that accommodate a multi-level class.

- We integrate school with home culture and with the greater community.

We strive for materials and activities that are relevant for a culturally diverse group and that help students to develop their self-esteem by valuing their unique cultural heritages. We seek to involve students in the community and the community with schools by providing and encouraging activities and projects that relate to community life and that put students into interaction with community representatives. This active involvement is integral to the development of students' content-area knowledge and language.

In order to reach toward these goals and implement these four kinds of integration, we have used integrated thematic units as the organizational basis for *Making Connections*. Our themes are arrived at in a variety of ways: some, like "Choosing Foods," have very concrete connections among the sections of the units. Others, like "Waves," make more metaphorical connections among sections that treat very different aspects of the theme. In all the units, students will make connections across content areas and will revisit themes and use and re-use the language of themes in different ways. Each unit provides multi-level information and experiences that integrate language with one or more content areas and includes the following features:

Learning strategies. In each unit, we incorporate strategies to help students with their language and content area learning. We encourage teachers and students to be aware of the applicability of these strategies in new learning situations. Our goal is to create active, capable, self-starting learners.

Cooperative learning. Cooperative learning has been shown to be effective in facilitating both student learning and successful cross-cultural, multi-level student integration. Each unit uses a variety of cooperative groupings and activities to achieve these goals.

Language Focus. Language is learned best in a meaningful, useful context. In *Making Connections*, students use language to accomplish real tasks, many of which they have chosen themselves from activity menus. From these meaningful contexts, many opportunities arise to teach language concepts as they are needed. Both the student text and the teacher's edition contain suggestions for taking advantage of opportunities for teaching language features as these opportunities arise.

Content-area experiences in science, social studies, and literature. We have chosen three content areas for focus in *Making Connections* because of their importance to student success and because of the importance of language to success in these areas. In science, we introduce the language of science (and frequently mathematics language as well) through offering authentic scientific experiences using materials that are accessible to an ESOL teacher. In social studies, we take advantage of the multicultural nature of ESOL classes to introduce the processes of the social sciences. We have provided literature in a variety of genres to enhance content-area learning. As students begin to learn the language, they need to talk about and create their own literary works.

Choices for teachers and students in multicultural, multilevel classrooms. Every ESOL class is a multilevel, multicultural class. In order to meet the needs of these diverse groups and in order to empower both teachers and students, *Making Connections* offers many choices. Teachers can choose among the many activities in the units to provide experiences most appropriate to their classes and can sequence these activities as needed. They can also individualize by choosing different activities for different students within the class. Each unit includes an activity menu of experiences and projects that will help students to integrate and apply the material from the unit. Both teacher and students can make choices among these culminating events to suit them to student interests, level of ability, and needs. Related literary selections following each unit offer additional choices for teachers and students interested in reading extensions.

Since we are teachers as well as authors, we know that the most important aspect of your instructional program is what happens between teacher and student. We have tried to develop a program that offers teachers and students many choices of activities, resources, and ideas that provide chances to interact, learn, and grow. We hope *Making Connections* helps students learn what they need to experience success in school as well as in life. We welcome teacher feedback and students' responses to *Making Connections*.

The authors

= additional activities available on **Making Connections CD-ROM**.

Contents

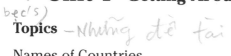

Unit 1 - Getting Around School

Topics

Unit 2 - Spending Free Time

Topics

Unit 3 - Counting Dollars and Cents

Topics

Unit 4 - Choosing Clothes

Topics

Unit 5 - Checking the Weather

Topics

Unit 6 - Making Journeys

Topics

Unit 7 - Solving Problems 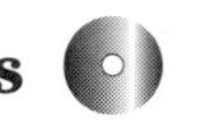

Topics

Unit 8 - Exploring Diversity 

Topics

MAKING CONNECTIONS Book 1

 = additional activities available on **Making Connections CD-ROM**.

FUNCTIONS	STRUCTURES	STUDY STRATEGIES
Introducing Yourself and Other People Telling Where People Are From Telling the Time Locating Places Asking and Answering Questions About Class Schedules Expressing Likes and Dislikes	Present Tense: *be, like* "Wh" Questions: *where, what* Yes/No Questions: Present Tense Subject Pronouns Possessive Adjectives	Selective Listening Reading a Class Schedule Making a Chart
Expressing Likes and Dislikes Comparing Likes and Dislikes Making and Responding to Suggestions Describing Daily Routines	Present Tense: Affirmative Present Tense: Negative Yes/No Questions: Affirmative and Negative *Let's . . .* (formulaic) *I'd love to . . .* (formulaic)	Classifying Making a Venn Diagram Evaluating Making a Cluster Diagram Reading a Chart
Identifying Amounts of Money Asking and Answering Questions About Prices Guessing Comparing Prices Ordering Food	"Wh" Questions: *who, which, how much* Present Tense Comparative Forms of Adjectives *I'd like . . .* (formulaic) *That'll be . . .* (formulaic)	Making a Chart Selective Listening  Selective Reading
Identifying Clothes Describing Clothes Expressing Likes and Dislikes Comparing Clothes Giving Reasons Making Plans	"Wh" Questions: *what, which, why* Present Tense Present Continuous Object Pronouns Comparative Forms of Adjectives *Because* Future with *be going to*	Selective Listening Making a Chart  Interviewing Quickwriting Writing a Poem

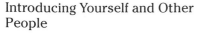

MAKING CONNECTIONS *Book 1*

FUNCTIONS	STRUCTURES	STUDY STRATEGIES
Identifying Weather Conditions Predicting the Weather Describing Weather Conditions Comparing Temperatures Guessing	Present Continuous Future with *be going to* Simple Past Comparative Form of Adjectives Superlative Form of Adjectives	Reading a Map Reading a Line Graph Making a Story Map Selective Listening
Locating Countries Identifying Possible Ways to Travel Evaluating Forms of Transportation Describing Places Giving Reasons Locating Places in North America Planning a Trip	Present Tense *can/can't* Questions with *can* Superlative Form of Adjectives Adverbs of Manner "Wh" Questions: *what, where, when, why, how* Future with *will*	Reading a Map Classifying Making a Chart Using Pictures Analyzing Using a Formula Making a Cluster Diagram
Identifying Problems and Solutions Making Predictions (Guessing) Describing a Sequence of Events in the Past Guessing Suggesting Possible Solutions Giving Instructions	Simple Past *Could/Couldn't* "Wh" Questions: *who, what, where, why, how* Commands	Using Pictures Selective Reading Making a Plot Profile
Identifying Similarities and Differences Giving Information About Yourself and Others Describing a Sequence of Events in the Past	Present Tense Simple Past *and, but* "Wh" Questions: *who, what, where, when, why*	Making a Venn Diagram Reading a Chart Making a Story Map Selective Reading Using Context Taking Notes in a Chart Interviewing Making a Cluster Diagram

Acknowledgments

The authors want to thank colleagues, students, and teachers from whom we have learned much and who have offered strong and encouraging support for this project. We thank Chris Foley, Roseanne Mendoza, Nancy Mann, Elaine Leary, and Lisa McLaughlin for their support in the development and production of this project and for weathering with us the storms and challenges of doing something so new. Our expert office staff—Josie Cressman and Sherrie Tindle—provided intelligent and efficient assistance always accompanied by friendship, and we are appreciative. We also want to thank family members—Erin, Dierdre, and Jim Stack; Kevin and Sean O'Brien, and Joel and Tom Reed—for their love and support during this project.

The publisher and authors wish to thank the following teachers who pilot tested the *Making Connections* program. Their valuable feedback on teaching with these materials greatly improved the final product. We are grateful to all of them for their dedication and commitment to teaching with the program in a prepublication format.

Elias S. Andrade and Gudrun Draper
James Monroe High School
North Hills, CA

Nadine Bagel
Benjamin Franklin Middle School
San Francisco, CA

Kate Bamberg
Newcomer High School
San Francisco, CA

Kate Charles
Sycamore Junior High School
Anaheim, CA

Anne Elmkies, Irene Killian, and Kay Stark
Hartford Public Schools
Hartford, CT

Genoveva Goss
Alhambra High School
Alhambra, CA

Margaret Hartman
Lewisville High School
Lewisville, TX

Carmen N. Jimenez
Intermediate School 184
New York, NY

Rob Lamont and Judith D. Clark
Trimble Technical High School
Fort Worth, TX

Judi Levin
Northridge Middle School
Northridge, CA

Ligita Longo
Spring Woods High School
Houston, TX

Mary Makena
Rancho Alamitas High School
Garden Grove, CA

Alexandra M. McHugh
Granby, CT

Beatrice W. Miranda
Leal Middle School
San Antonio, TX

Doris Partan
Longfellow School
Cambridge, MA

Jane Pierce
Douglas MacArthur High School
San Antonio, TX

Cynthia Prindle
Thomas Jefferson High School
San Antonio, TX

Sydney Rodrigues
Doig Intermediate School
Garden Grove, CA

Cecelia Ryan
Monte Vista High School
Spring Valley, CA

Patsy Thompson
Gwinnett Vocational Center
Lawrenceville, GA

Fran Venezia
North Dallas High School
Dallas, TX

The publisher and authors would also like to thank the following people who reviewed the *Making Connections* program at various stages of development. Their insights and suggestions are much appreciated.

Suzanne Barton
Fort Worth Independent School District
Forth Worth, TX

Keith Buchanan
Fairfax County Public Schools
Fairfax, VA

Carlos Byfield
San Diego City College
San Diego, CA

John Croes
Lowell High School
Lowell, MA

Flo Decker
El Paso, TX

Lynn Dehart
North Dallas High School
Dallas, TX

Cecilia Esquer
El Monte High School
El Monte, CA

Marge Gianelli
Canutillo Independent School District
El Paso, TX

Nora Harris
Harlandale Independent School District
San Antonio, TX

Richard Hurst
Holbrook High School
Holbrook, AZ

Betty J. Mace-Matluck
Southwest Educational Development Laboratory
Austin, TX

Jacqueline Moase-Burke
Oakland Independent School District
Oakland, MI

Jeanne Perrin
Boston Public Schools
Boston, MA

Ron Reese
Long Beach Unified School District
Long Beach, CA

Linda Sasser
Alhambra School District
Alhambra, CA

Donna Sievers
Garden Grove Unified School District
Garden Grove, CA

Stephen F. Sloan
James Monroe High School
North Hills, CA

Dorothy Taylor
Adult Learning Center
Buffalo Public Schools
Buffalo, NY

Beth Winningham
James Monroe High School
North Hills, CA

Components of the Making Connections Program

In addition to the student text, each level of Making Connections includes the following components:

Teacher's Extended Edition

This Teacher's Extended Edition provides:

- an introduction to the thematic, integrated teaching approach
- a description of several approaches to presenting literature selections
- a guide to the study strategies that appear in the student book
- detailed teaching suggestions for each activity
- suggestions for extension activities
- listening scripts

Workbooks

Workbooks provide additional practice in using the vocabulary, language functions, language structures, and study strategies introduced in each of the thematic units. Workbook activities can be used in class or assigned as homework.

CD-ROM

This lively, fun, user-friendly program features highly interactive units that parallel the student text. Students engage in sentence completion, interact with videos, create notes from a variety of sources, and complete graphs and charts. Also included is a writing area, an additional language practice section, and printing scorecards for each unit. The program is colorful, easy to navigate and offers a help feature on every screen.

Literacy Masters

Literacy Masters provide special support for preliterate students. These materials are designed for students who enter the program at the Preproduction or Early Production stage. (Students who have only minimal comprehension of English.) The materials correspond with the units of *Making Connections I* and are very useful in multilevel classes.

The Teacher's Guide to the Heinle & Heinle ESL Program

The Heinle & Heinle ESL Program consists of the two series: *Making Connections 1, 2, and 3*, and *Voices in literature, Bronze, Silver, and Gold*, which can be used independently or together. The Teacher's Guide th the Heinle & Heinle ESL Program provides much practical advice and strategies for using the two series together. In this guide, classroom practitioners will learn how to take advantage of the revisitation of terms, themes, content and literature are organized thematically, students can continuously relate and analyze academic concepts and literary works. This Teacher's Guide also offers strategies for providing instruction to students at many levels—from beginning English language proficiency to advanced levels of content-based and literature-based instruction. A technology section describes how instructors can use electronic support, such as e-mail and software, to expand on the activities found in *Making Connections* and *Voices in Literature.*

Assessment Program

The Assessment Program consists of several components and accommodates a range of assessment philosophies and formats. Included are:

- a portfolio assessment kit, complete with a teacher's guide to using portfolios and forms for student and teacher evaluation
- two "progress checks" per unit
- one comprehensive test per unit

Transparencies

Color Transparencies provide enlargements of visuals from the student texts. Many teachers find it helpful to view visuals with the students as they point out details. They may also write on pages using blank overlay transparencies.

Activity Masters

Reproducible activity masters support activities from the student book by providing write-on forms and graphic organizers for student's use. Activities for use with these masters consistently promote active student roles in engaging experiences.

Tape Program

Audio Tapes provide opportunities for group and individual extended practice with the series materials. The tapes contain all the listening activities included in the student texts. Scripts of the recorded material are included in the Teacher's Extended Edition.

MAKING CONNECTIONS 1:

An Integrated Approach to Learning English

Language Focus

- This is Fernando. He is from Mexico.
- This is Marta. She is from Russia.

Getting Around School

1. Listen

a. Classwork. Listen and find the person.

b. On your own. Where are these students from? Mark your answer in a chart like this.

Where are they from?						
	Colombia	Japan	Haiti	Iran	Mexico	Russia
Fernando					✓	
Marta						✓
Satoshi						
Nadine						
Ali						
Claudia						

Language Focus

- Fernando is from Mexico.
- Marta is from Russia.

c. Compare answers with your classmates.

He is from Mexico.

giới thiệu Chính bạn

2. Introduce Yourself

a. Pairwork. Introduce yourself to a partner.

A: Hi. My name is Fernando.

I'm from Mexico.

B: Hi. I'm Marta.

I'm from Russia.

Language Focus

A: Hi. My name is Fernando. I'm from Mexico.

B: Hi. I'm Marta. I'm from Russia.

I'm = I am

b. Introduce your partner to the class.

This is Fernando. He's from Mexico.
This is Marta. She's from Russia.

3. Play a Game

a. Classwork. Write your first name on a card like this:

Maria

Give your card to your teacher.

b. On your own. Introduce yourself to nine classmates. Write their names in a chart like this.

Maria	*Lan*	*Alisha*
Anh	*Rocco*	*Fernando*
Ben	*Nicole*	*Ahmad*

c. Follow your teacher's instructions to play a game of bingo.

Language Focus

- This is Fernando. He's from Mexico.
- This is Marta. She's from Russia.

He's = He is
She's = She is

4. Analyze

a. Pairwork. Study these pictures and answer the questions on page 6.

In homeroom

In the cafeteria

In English class

In gym class

In science class

In history class

Language Focus

Q: Where is Tran at two o'clock?

A: In science class.

In art class

In math class

In the hallway

Where is Tran at . . . . .

seven forty-five?	*in homeroom*
eight?	
nine ten?	
ten thirty?	
eleven forty-five?	
twelve thirty?	
one ten?	
two?	
two fifty-five?	

b. Compare answers with your classmates.

5. Write

a. Pairwork. Write Tran's class schedule in a chart like this. Use the information on pages 4–5.

Tran's Class Schedule		
Period	**Time**	**Class**
Homeroom	7:30–7:50	*homeroom*
First Period	7:55–8:50	*English*
Second Period	8:55–9:50	
Third Period	9:55–10:50	
Fourth Period	10:55–11:50	
Fifth Period	11:55–12:50	
Sixth Period	12:55–1:50	
Seventh Period	1:55–2:50	

Language Focus

- Tran's first-period class is English.
- Tran's second-period class is ________________.

b. Compare answers with another pair.

A: What is Tran's first -period class?
B: English .

Language Focus

Q: What is Tran's first-period class?
A: English.

6. Write

a. On your own. Write your schedule for today in a chart like this.

My Schedule		
Period	**Time**	**Class**
Homeroom		
First Period		
Second Period		
Third Period		
Fourth Period		
Fifth Period		
Sixth Period		
Seventh Period		

Language Focus

A: What is your first-period class?
B: English. What is your first-period class?
A: English.

b. Pairwork. Compare schedules with a partner.

7. Interview

Cuộc phỏng vấn

a. Classwork. Add your name to a chart on the board.

Name	art	English	gym	history	math	music	science
Mei		✓					

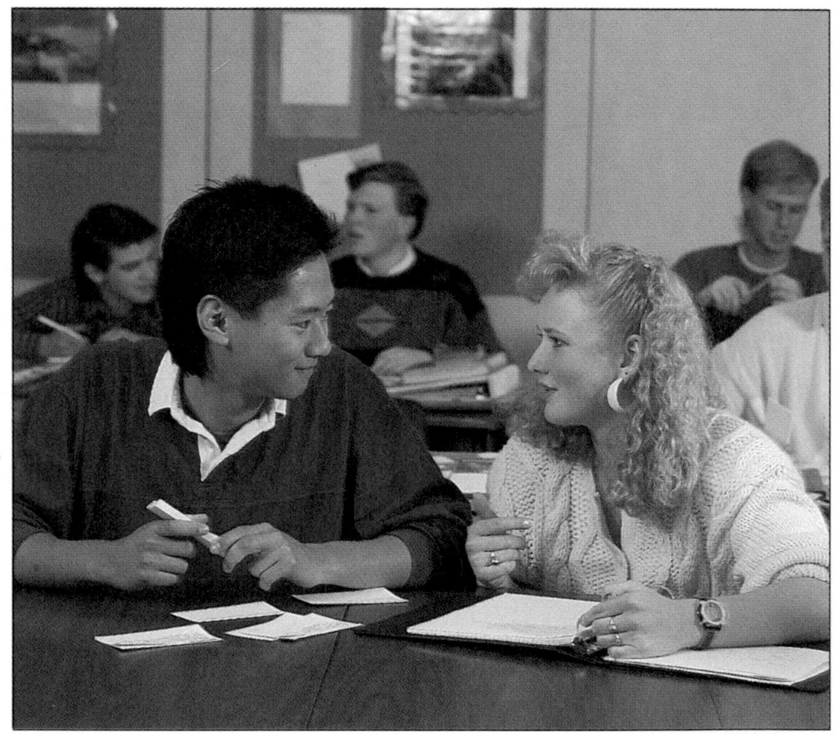

b. Pairwork. Interview a partner. Add your partner's answer to the chart on the board.

A: What is your favorite class?

B: read book and write. What is your favorite class?

A: Speaking and math.

Language Focus

Q: What is your favorite class?

A: Science.

c. Classwork. Count your classmates' answers. Write the numbers in a chart like this:

Favorite Class	Number of Students
art	*2*
English	*2*
gym	*3*
history	*1*
math	*4*
music	*2*
science	*3*

d. Pairwork. Which class is the most popular? Which class is the least popular? Write your answers on a line like this:

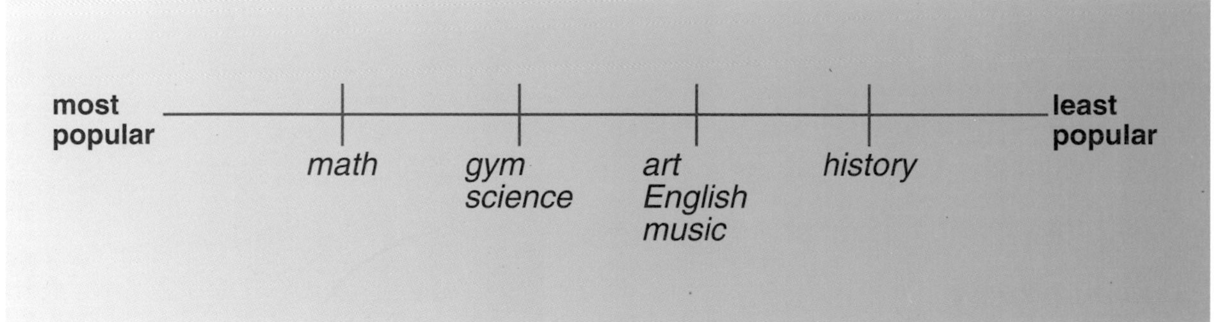

e. Compare charts with your classmates.

8. Explore Your School

Classwork. Answer the questions on page 11. Then take a trip around your school and answer the questions again.

▼ Nurse's office

Music room ▲

Library/media center ▲

Auditorium ▼

Gym ▲

PLACES AT YOUR SCHOOL				
Questions	**Answers**			
	Before your trip		**After your trip**	
Does your school have an auditorium?	Yes	No	Yes	No
Does your school have a gym?	Yes	No	Yes	No
Does your school have an outdoor track?	Yes	No	Yes	No
Does your school have a woodshop?	Yes	No	Yes	No
Does your school have a library/media center?	Yes	No	Yes	No
Does your school have a cafeteria?	Yes	No	Yes	No
Does your school have a computer lab?	Yes	No	Yes	No
Does your school have a science lab?	Yes	No	Yes	No
Does your school have a nurse's office?	Yes	No	Yes	No
Does your school have a music room?	Yes	No	Yes	No
____________________	Yes	No	Yes	No

Computer lab ▲

▼Science lab

Outdoor track ▲

▲ Woodshop

9. Recall

a. Groupwork. On your trip around the school, did you see anyone doing these things? Where? Write your answers in a chart.

Writing ▼

▲ Working in a group

Playing basketball ▲

Did you see anyone . . . ?	Yes	No	If yes, where?
reading			
writing			
working in a group			
writing on the blackboard			
standing in line			
playing basketball			
using a computer			

b. Compare charts with another group.

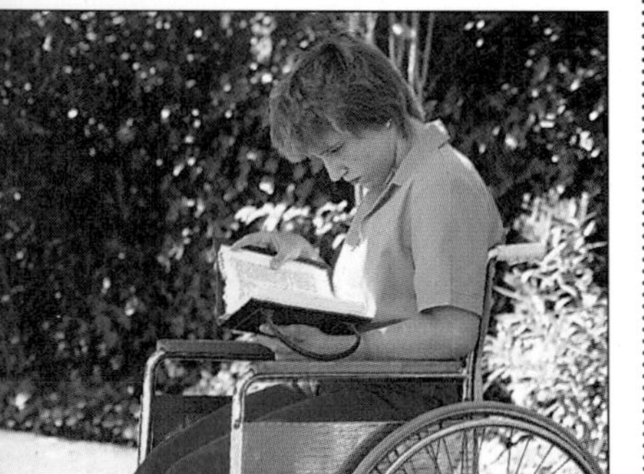

Reading ▲

Using a computer ▲

▲ Writing on the blackboard

▲ Standing in line

10. Interview

a. Pairwork. Interview your partner.

A: Do you like to *read* ____________________?

B: Yes I do. (No, I don't).

Do you like to ____________?	Yes	No
read	✓	
play basketball		
work in a group		
write		
stand in line		
use a computer		

b. Tell the class about your partner.

My partner likes to ____________________.

Language Focus

Q: Do you lke to read?

A: Yes, I do. (No, I don't.)

Language Focus

- My partner likes to read.
- Mei likes to play basketball.

Activity Menu

Choose one of the following activities to do.

1. Take Photographs
Take photographs of students in different places at your school. Ask your classmates to write captions for the photographs.

2. Draw a map
Draw a map of your school for new students. Choose important places at your school and locate them on your map.

3. Go on a Scavenger Hunt
Find these things at your school. Tell where you found each thing. Then compare ideas with your classmates.

These students are playing badminton in the school gym.

What	Where
▪ a basketball hoop	*in the gym*
▪ a drinking fountain	
▪ a wall map	
▪ a microscope	
▪ a copy machine	
▪ an atlas (book of maps)	
▪ a flag	
▪ ____________________	

4. Make a Class Map

Where are your classmates from? Locate these countries on a world map. Use small flags, pins, or other markers to identify each person's native country.

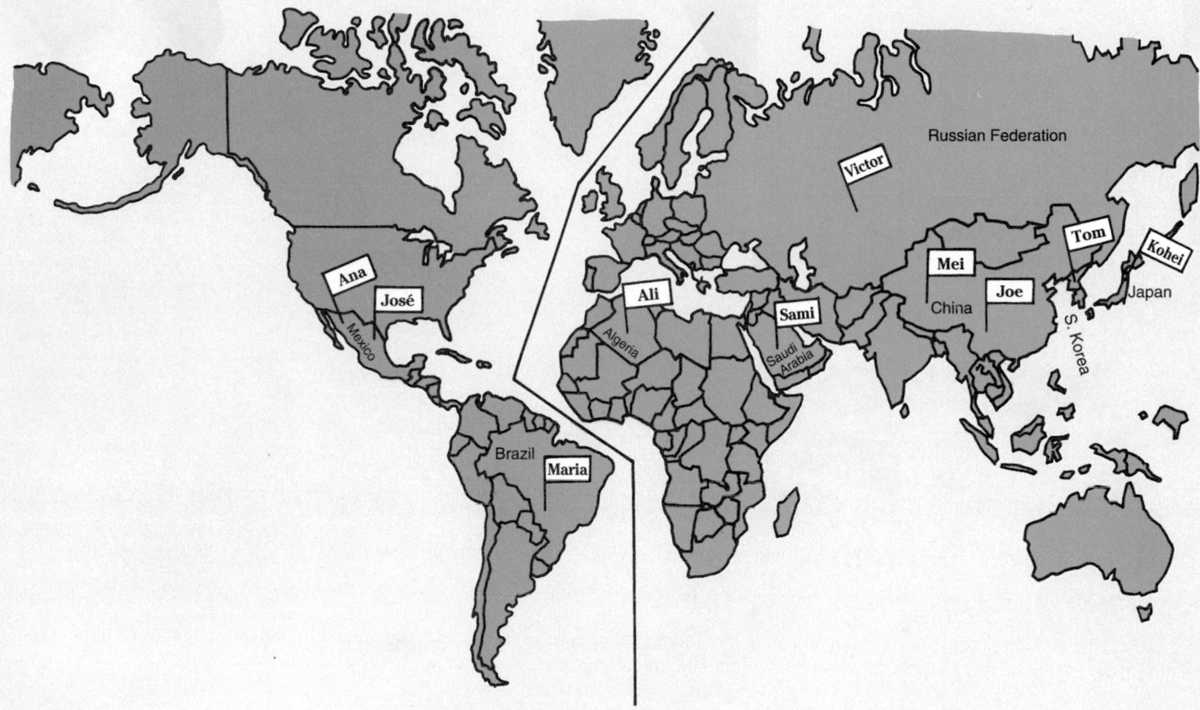

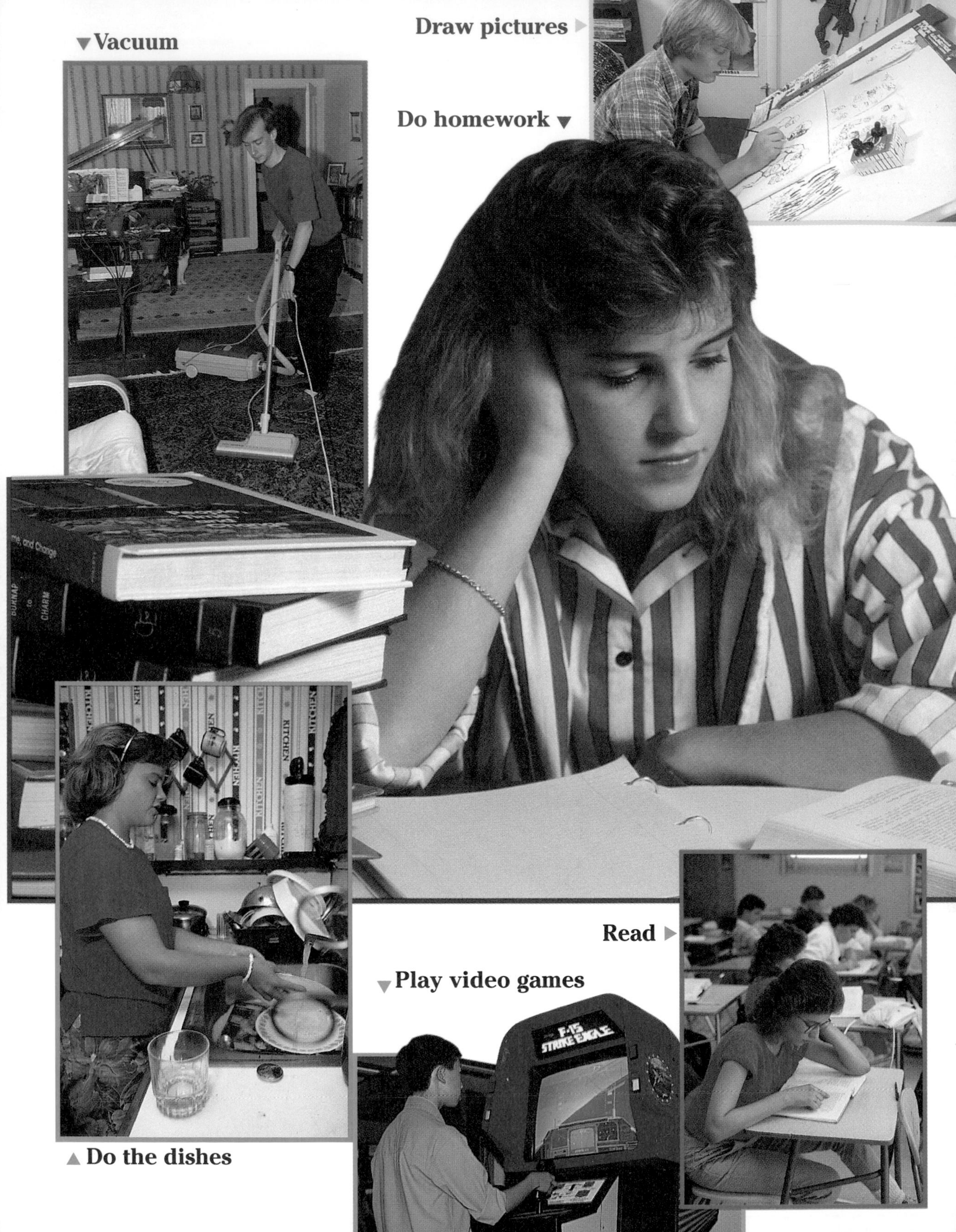

▼ Vacuum

Draw pictures ▶

Do homework ▼

▲ Do the dishes

▼ Play video games

Read ▶

Spending Free Time

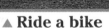

▼ Take tests

1. Classify

Classwork. Add these activities to a chart like this.

School Activities	Housework	Free Time Activities
		play video games

▲ Ride a bike

◀ Cook

▲ Read

Language Focus

- I like to listen to music in my free time.
- I like to play soccer.
- I like to ________ .

Listen

Classwork. Listen and find the person.

Listen to music ▼

Play the guitar ▶

◂ **Watch TV**

Play volleyball ▾

Play soccer ▴

▾ **Talk on the telephone**

▴ **Go shopping**

What do you like to do in your free time?

I like to ______________________________.

3. Classify

a. Pairwork. Put these activities into two groups. Then answer the questions below.

ride a bike	play soccer
play volleyball	draw
listen to music	play the guitar
go shopping	

Indoor/Outdoor Activities

play volleyball

Outdoor Activities

ride a bike

Language Focus

- I like to play soccer.
- My partner likes to ride a bike.

What do you like to do outdoors?

I like to . . . . .

My partner likes to . . . . .

What do you like to do indoors?

I like to . . . . .

My partner likes to . . . . .

b. Pairwork. Put these outdoor activities into two groups:

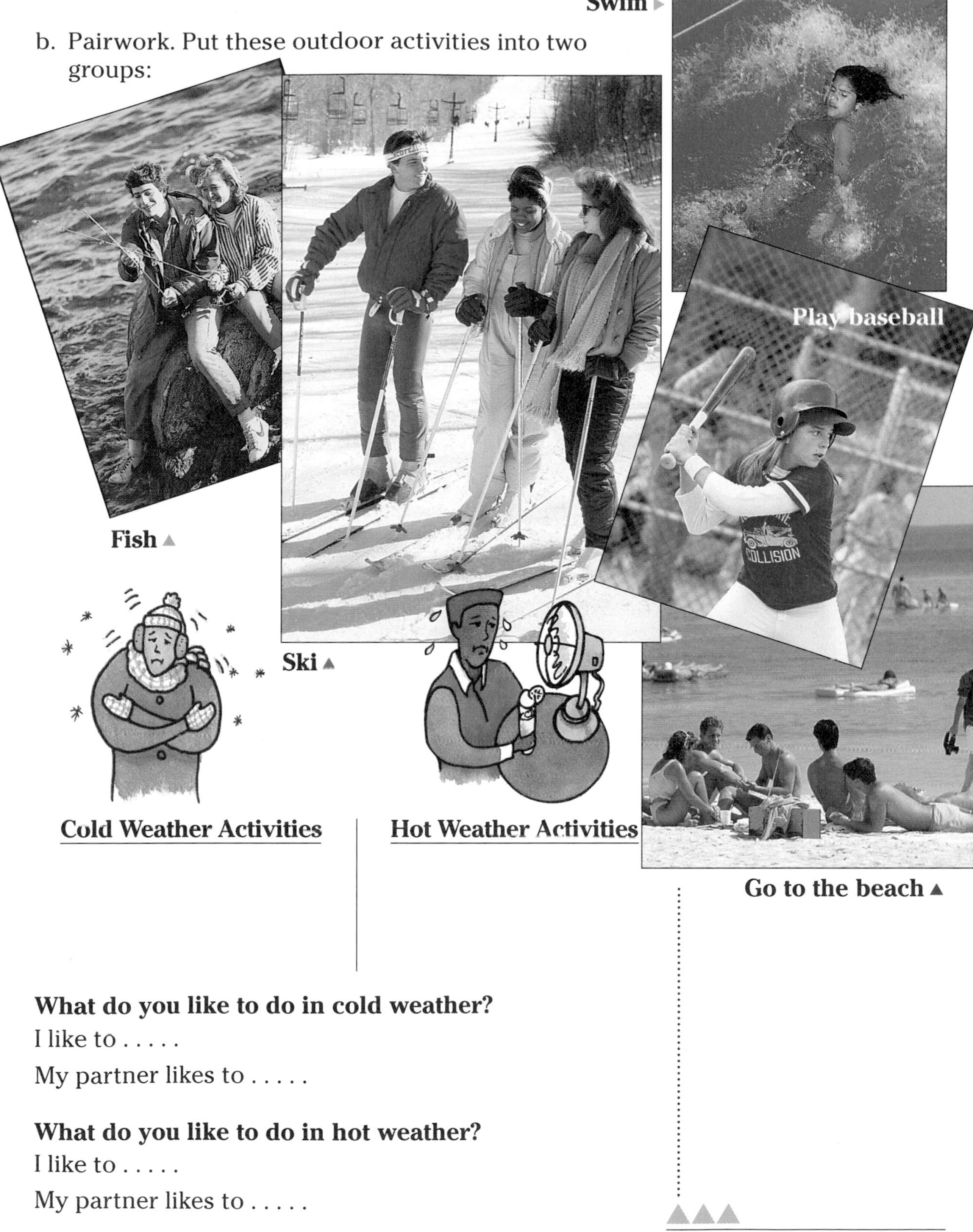

Cold Weather Activities	Hot Weather Activities

What do you like to do in cold weather?

I like to . . . . .

My partner likes to . . . . .

What do you like to do in hot weather?

I like to . . . . .

My partner likes to . . . . .

4. Play a Game

Materials: two index cards per student

a. Pairwork. Interview your partner.

Q: What do you like to do in your free time?
A: I like to *play the guitar*.

b. Write your partner's answer on a card like this:

c. On another card, illustrate your partner's answer.

d. Get together in groups of 5 or 6. Follow your teacher's instructions to play a game called *Concentration.*

5. Interview

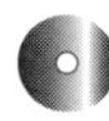

a. Classwork. Listen and record each person's answer in a chart like this.

Do you like to listen to music?	Yes, I do.	No, I don't.
Do you like to talk on the telephone?	Yes, I do.	No, I don't.
Do you like to play soccer?	Yes, I do.	No, I don't.
Do you like to go shopping?	Yes, I do.	No, I don't.
Do you like to watch TV?	Yes, I do.	No, I don't.

b. Pairwork. Interview a partner.

▲ Dance

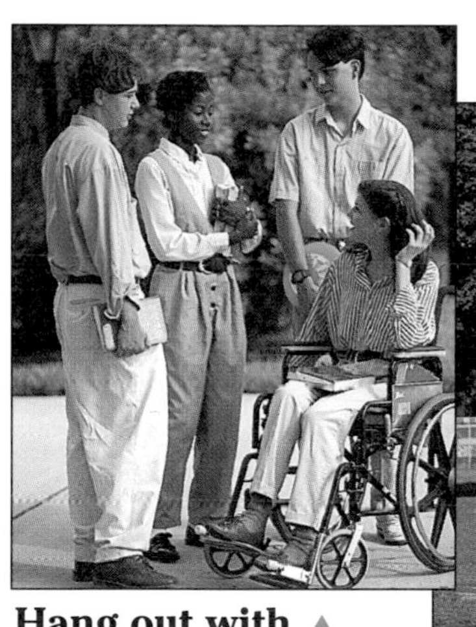

Hang out with friends ▲

Play basketball ▶

Go to the movies ▼

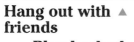

Do you like to ________?	Yes, I do	No, I don't
play basketball	✓	
dance		
go to the movies		
hang out with friends		
________		
________		

Language Focus

Q: Do you like to play basketball?
A: Yes, I do. (No, I don't.)

c. Classwork. Make a class chart. Add information about your partner.

likes to dance	doesn't like to dance
Hanh	*Carl*
Don	*Magda*

likes to play basketball	doesn't like to play basketball

How many students like to dance? ______
How many students don't like to dance? ______
How many students like to play basketball? ______
How many students don't like to play basketball? ______

Language Focus

- Hanh likes to dance.
- Carl doesn't like to dance.

6. Interview

On your own. Find someone who *likes to cook*.
Write the person's name in a chart like this.

Find someone who ______.	
likes to cook	*Carl*
doesn't like to cook	*José*
likes to run	______
doesn't like to swim	______
likes to go to the beach	______
doesn't like to draw	______
______	______
______	______

Language Focus

A: Carl, do you like to cook?
B: Yes, I do.

A: José, do you like to cook?
C: No, I don't.

7. Compare

a. Pairwork. Ask your partner about free time activities. Together make a Venn Diagram like this:

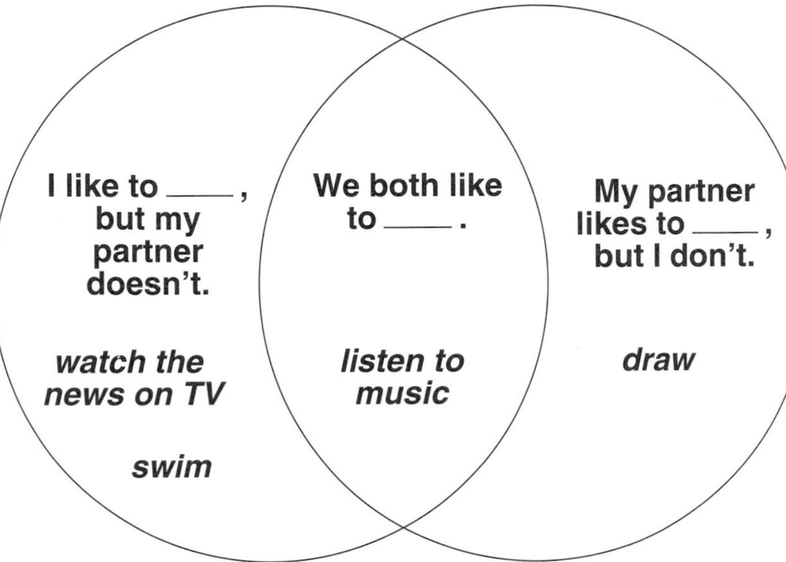
I like to ____, but my partner doesn't.
watch the news on TV
swim
We both like to ____.
listen to music
My partner likes to ____, but I don't.
draw

> ***Language Focus***
>
> **A:** Do you like to listen to music?
> **B:** Sure. What about you?
> **A:** I do, too.
> **B:** Do you like to swim?
> **A:** No, I don't. What about you?
> **B:** I really like to swim.

b. Write several sentences about you and your partner.

I like to swim but my partner doesn't
We both like to listen to music.

> ***Language Focus***
>
> - I like to swim, but Carlos doesn't.
> - We both like to listen to music.
> - Carlos likes to draw, but I don't.

a. Classwork. Listen and find the person.

Sure. I'd love to.

Sorry, I can't.

Great idea.

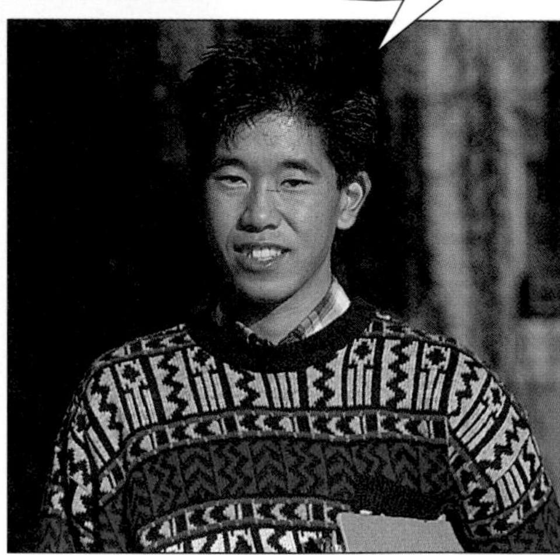

b. Pairwork. Practice these dialogues.

A: Do you want to *play basketball* ?
B: Sure. I'd love to. (Yes, I do. Great idea!)

A: Let's *go shopping* .
B: I'd love to, but I'm busy. (Sorry I can't.)

Language Focus

- Q: Do you want to play basketball?
  A: Sure. I'd love to.
- Q: Let's go shopping.
  A: I'd love to, but I'm busy.

9. Match

Pairwork. Choose words to complete the chant below.

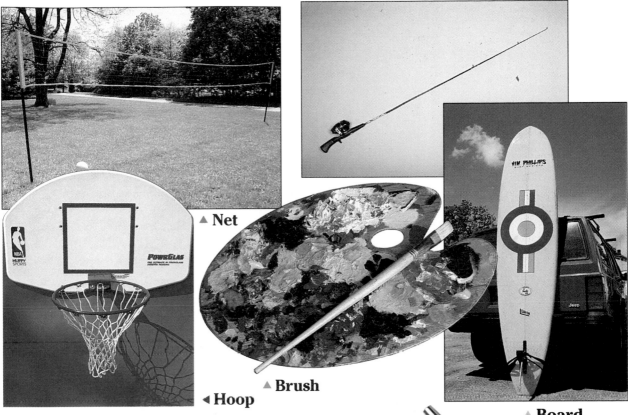

Pole

Net

Brush

Hoop

Board

Pen

I'd Love To 

I'd love to play basketball, but I don't have a *hoop*.

I'd love to write a letter, but I don't have a . . . .

I'd love to go fishing, but I don't have a . . . .

I'd love to paint a picture, but I don't have a . . . .

I'd love to go surfing, but I don't have a . . . .

I'd love to play volleyball, but I don't have a . . . .

But I do have . . . , so let's . . . .

10. Shared Reading

A hobby is something you do for fun. What are these people's hobbies?

Chess is popular at Junior High School 43 in Harlem, New York. Every day at lunch time, students get together to play chess. After school, some of the students play for three or four more hours.

Stephen Barton, a high school student in Hernando Beach, Florida, likes to build things—big things. He spent hundreds of hours at the computer and in the library, learning about submarines. Then he built this submarine in his basement.

11. Evaluate

Groupwork. Evaluate the hobbies in the reading. Tell what you think. Then add other hobbies to a chart like this.

Really Interesting Very Interesting Great ***	Interesting Fun **	Okay All right *	Boring —
building a submarine		*chess*	

Language Focus

- Chess is okay.
- _______ is boring.

Collecting stamps

Painting pictures

12. Make a Cluster Diagram

Classwork. Choose one hobby. Collect ideas about this hobby.

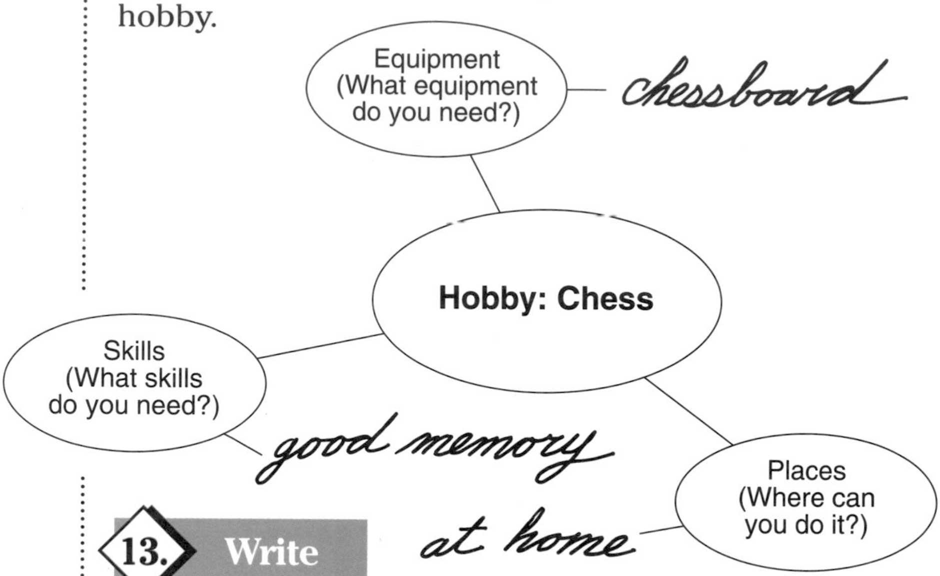

Equipment (What equipment do you need?) — chessboard

Hobby: Chess

Skills (What skills do you need?) — good memory

Places (Where can you do it?) — at home

13. Write

On your own. Tell about one of your hobbies.

a. Collect your ideas in a cluster diagram like this.

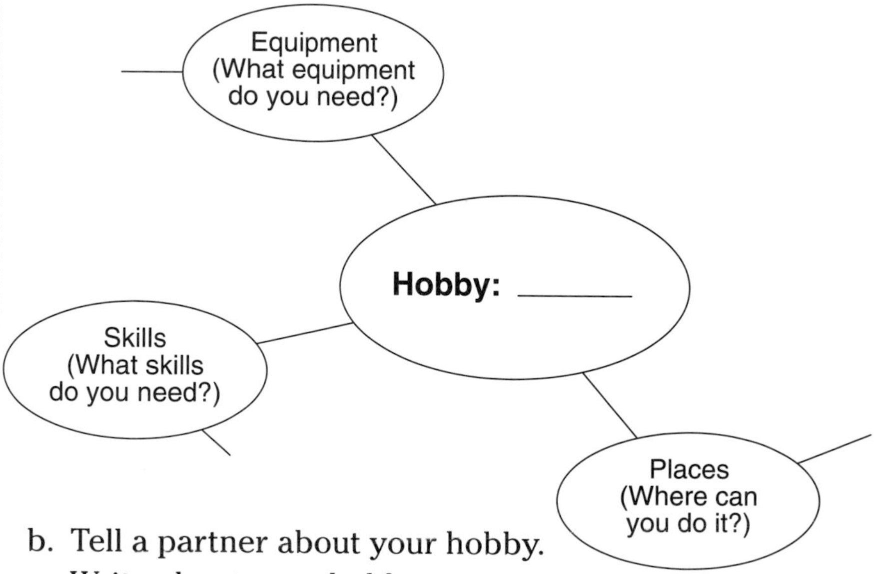

Equipment (What equipment do you need?)

Hobby: ______

Skills (What skills do you need?)

Places (Where can you do it?)

b. Tell a partner about your hobby.
c. Write about your hobby.
d. Share your writing with your classmates.

14. Read a Chart

a. Classwork. Read this chart and tell about Nina Todisco's daily schedule.

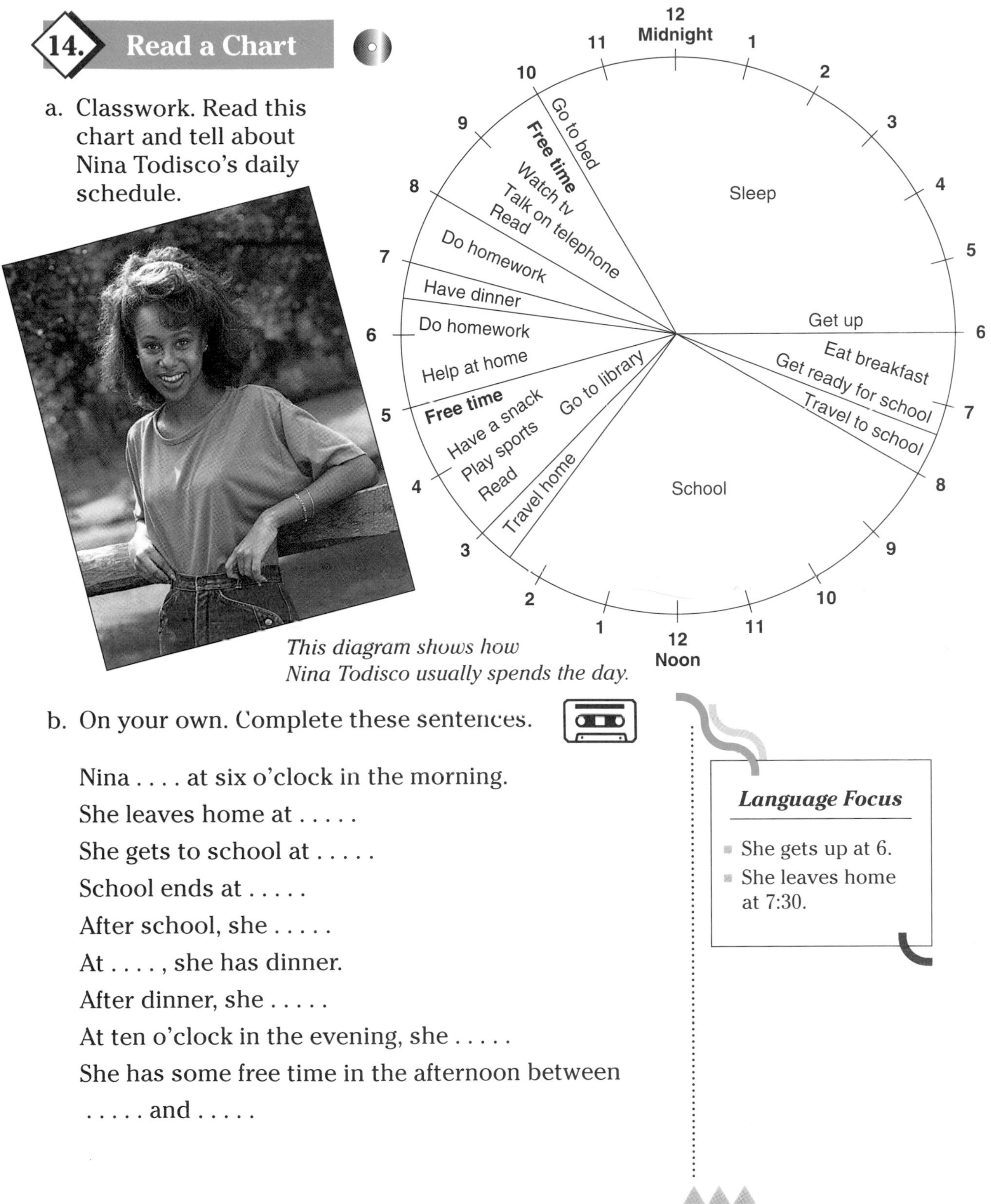

This diagram shows how Nina Todisco usually spends the day.

b. On your own. Complete these sentences.

Nina . . . . at six o'clock in the morning.

She leaves home at . . . . .

She gets to school at . . . . .

School ends at . . . . .

After school, she . . . . .

At . . . . , she has dinner.

After dinner, she . . . . .

At ten o'clock in the evening, she . . . . .

She has some free time in the afternoon between . . . . . and . . . . .

Language Focus

- She gets up at 6.
- She leaves home at 7:30.

She has some free time in the evening between
. . . . . and . . . . .

c. On your own. Answer these questions.

How much free time does Nina Todisco have each day?
What does she do in her free time?

15. Write

a. On your own. Write about your daily schedule.

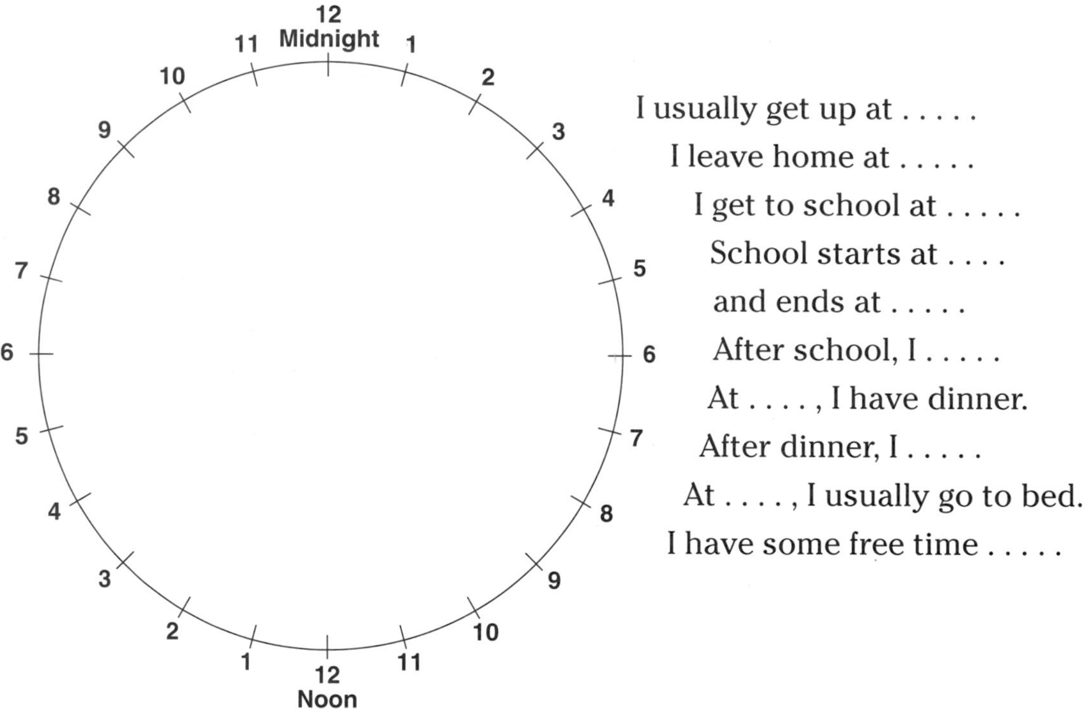

I usually get up at . . . . .
I leave home at . . . . .
I get to school at . . . . .
School starts at . . . .
and ends at . . . . .
After school, I . . . . .
At . . . . , I have dinner.
After dinner, I . . . . .
At . . . . , I usually go to bed.
I have some free time . . . . .

b. Draw a circle diagram. Show your daily schedule.

c. Exchange circle diagrams with a partner. Write about your partner's schedule.

My partner gets up at 6:30.

a. Classwork. Listen to the chant.

The Nothing to Do Blues

Hey man, I'm feeling blue.
There's nothing at all for me to do.

Play ball. Read a book.
What do you mean there's nothing to do?

b. Pairwork. Add your own words to the chant.

Nothing to Do

Hey man, I'm feeling blue.
There's nothing at all for me to do.

________________. ________________.

What do you mean there's nothing to do?

c. Read your chant to the class.

Activity Menu

Choose one of the following activities to do.

1. What do you do in your free time?
For one day, write down everything you do in your free time. Record your notes on a schedule like this:

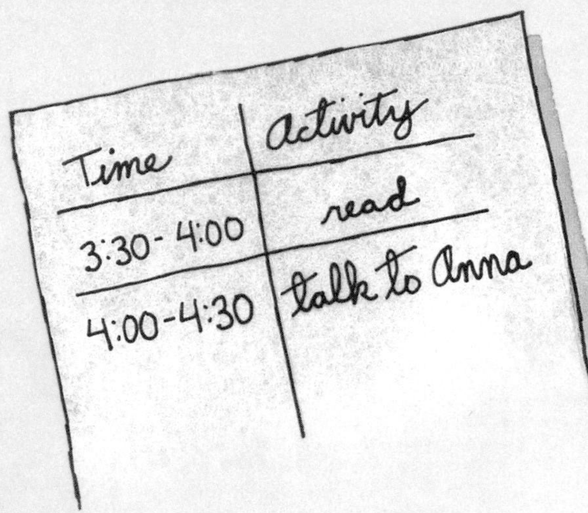

2. No School Today
What do you do on Saturday? Make a chart showing how you spend the day. Show how much free time you have. Tell what you do in your free time.

3. Interview
Ask three people—your friends or people in your family—about their free time. Ask: *What do you like to do in your free time? What don't you like to do in your free time?* Record their answers in a chart like this:

Name	Likes to do	Doesn't like to do

Write a summary of what you learned.

4. Make a Collage of Hobbies
Tell your classmates about one of your hobbies. Bring materials from home to show what you do. Then make a class collage of hobbies. Include information and pictures about each person's hobby.

5. Is It Dangerous?

Collect pictures of different sports. Evaluate each sport like this:

	Sports	
	bungee jumping	*tennis*
Very dangerous	✓	
Somewhat dangerous		
Slightly dangerous		
Not dangerous at all		

6. Play a Game

Teach your classmates how to play a card game or a board game like checkers.

7. Compare Daily Schedules

Compare your daily schedule with a partner's. Make a Venn Diagram like this:

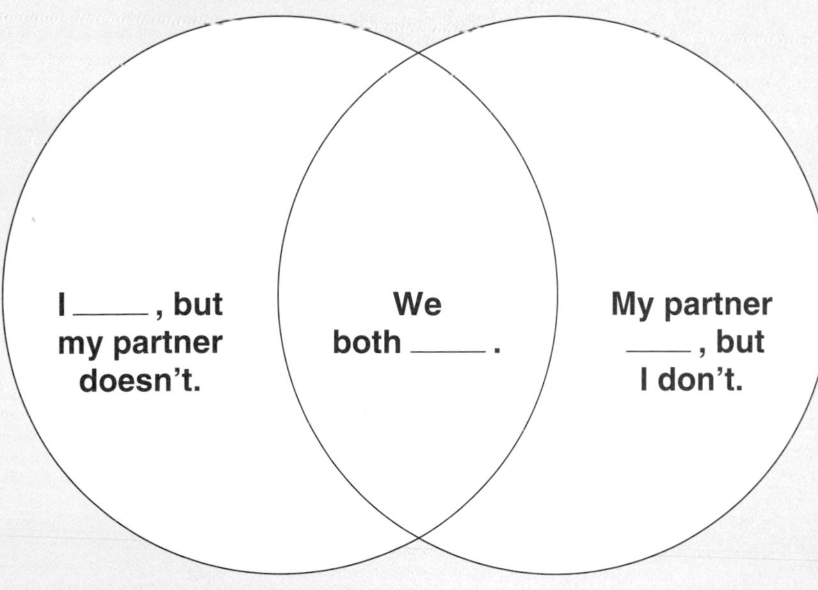
I ____, but my partner doesn't.
We both ____.
My partner ____, but I don't.

BROOK
BANK

Counting Dollars and Cents

▲ .25
Twenty-five cents
A quarter

▲ .10
Ten cents
A dime

▲ .05
Five cents
A nickel

▲ .01
One cent
A penny

Classwork. Listen and find the amount of money.

▲ **$1.00**
One dollar

▲ **$5.00**
Five dollars

▲ **$10.00**
Ten dollars

▲ **$20.00**
Twenty dollars

2. Identify

Pairwork. How much money is in each box? Write the amounts.

1

2

3

4

5

6

7

8

3. Listen

a. Classwork. Listen and find the number.

0 zero	1 one	2 two	3 three	4 four	5 five	6 six	7 seven
8 eight	9 nine	10 ten	11 eleven	12 twelve	13 thirteen	14 fourteen	15 fifteen
16 sixteen	17 seventeen	18 eighteen	19 nineteen	20 twenty	21 twenty-one	22 twenty-two	
30 thirty	40 forty	50 fifty	60 sixty	70 seventy	80 eighty	90 ninety	
100 one hundred		1000 one thousand					

b. Classwork. Listen and find the number.

thirteen	thirty
fourteen	forty
fifteen	fifty
sixteen	sixty
seventeen	seventy
eighteen	eighty
nineteen	ninety

4. Match

Pairwork. Find these amounts of money on page 41.

1. Five dollars and fifteen cents.
2. Two dollars and thirty cents.
3. Three dollars and fifty cents.
4. Fifty-seven cents.
5. One dollar and eighty cents.
6. Twenty-six cents.

a.
b.
c.
d.
e.
f.

5. Listen

Classwork. Listen and write the price.

A: Excuse me. How much does this dictionary cost?
B: Twelve dollars and ninety-five cents.
A: Thanks.

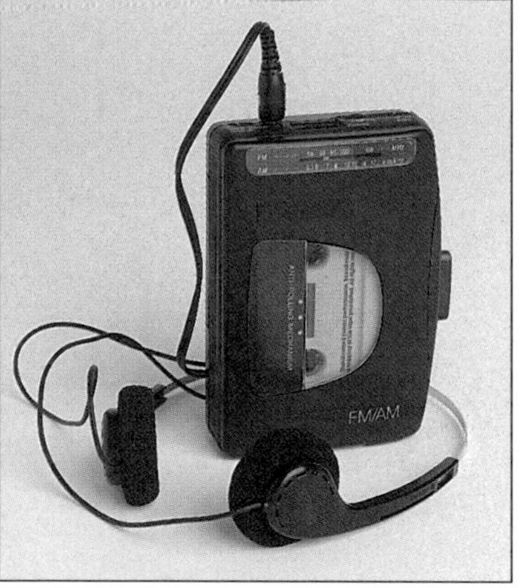

Dictionary **Walkman** **Watch**

> ***Language Focus***
>
> Q: How much does this dictionary cost?
> A: Twelve dollars and ninety-five cents.

Backpack **Pen** **Calculator**

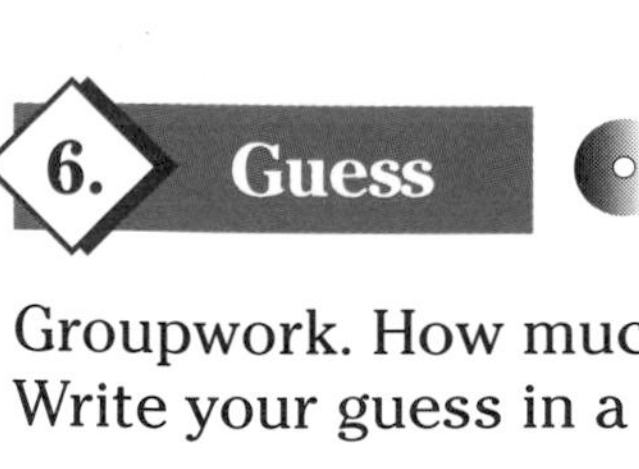

6. Guess

Groupwork. How much do you think these items cost? Write your guess in a chart.

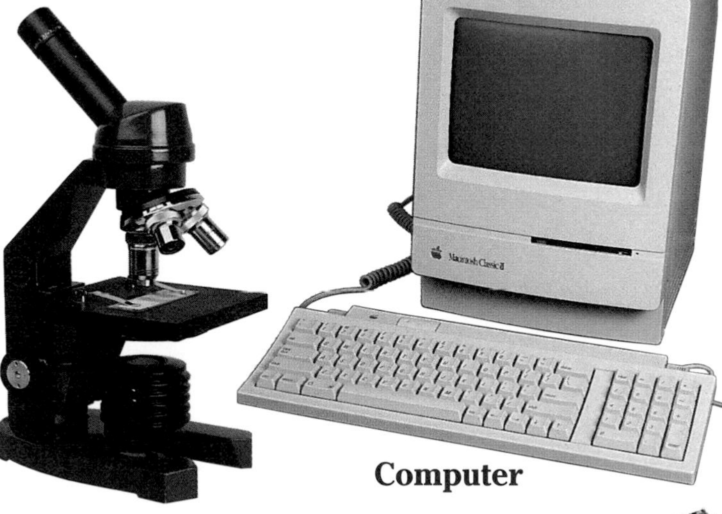

Computer

Microscope

Dictionary

Globe

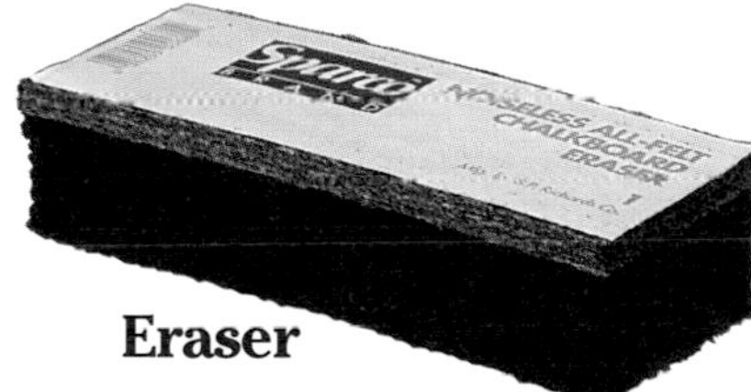

Eraser

Notebook

Item	Price	
	Guess	Actual
microscope		
computer		
dictionary		
eraser		
notebook		
globe		

b. Compare your guesses with the actual prices on page 59.

Language Focus

- I think the notebook costs about one dollar.
- We think the microscope costs five hundred dollars.

7. Compare

Pairwork. Which is cheaper? Circle your guesses in a chart like this.

Which is cheaper, the _______ or the _______ ?	
1. basketball	soccer ball
2. ice skates	roller blades
3. music CD	music cassette
4. shampoo	toothpaste
5. roll of film	blank videotape
6. 19" color TV	VCR

▲ Soccer ball

▲ Basketball

▼ Roller blades

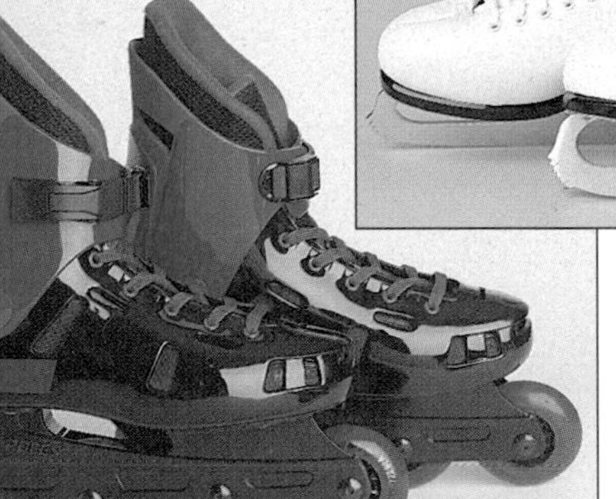

Ice skates ▲

Language Focus

Q: Which is cheaper, the baseball or the soccer ball?
A: The baseball.

Baseball $7.50

Soccer ball $24.95

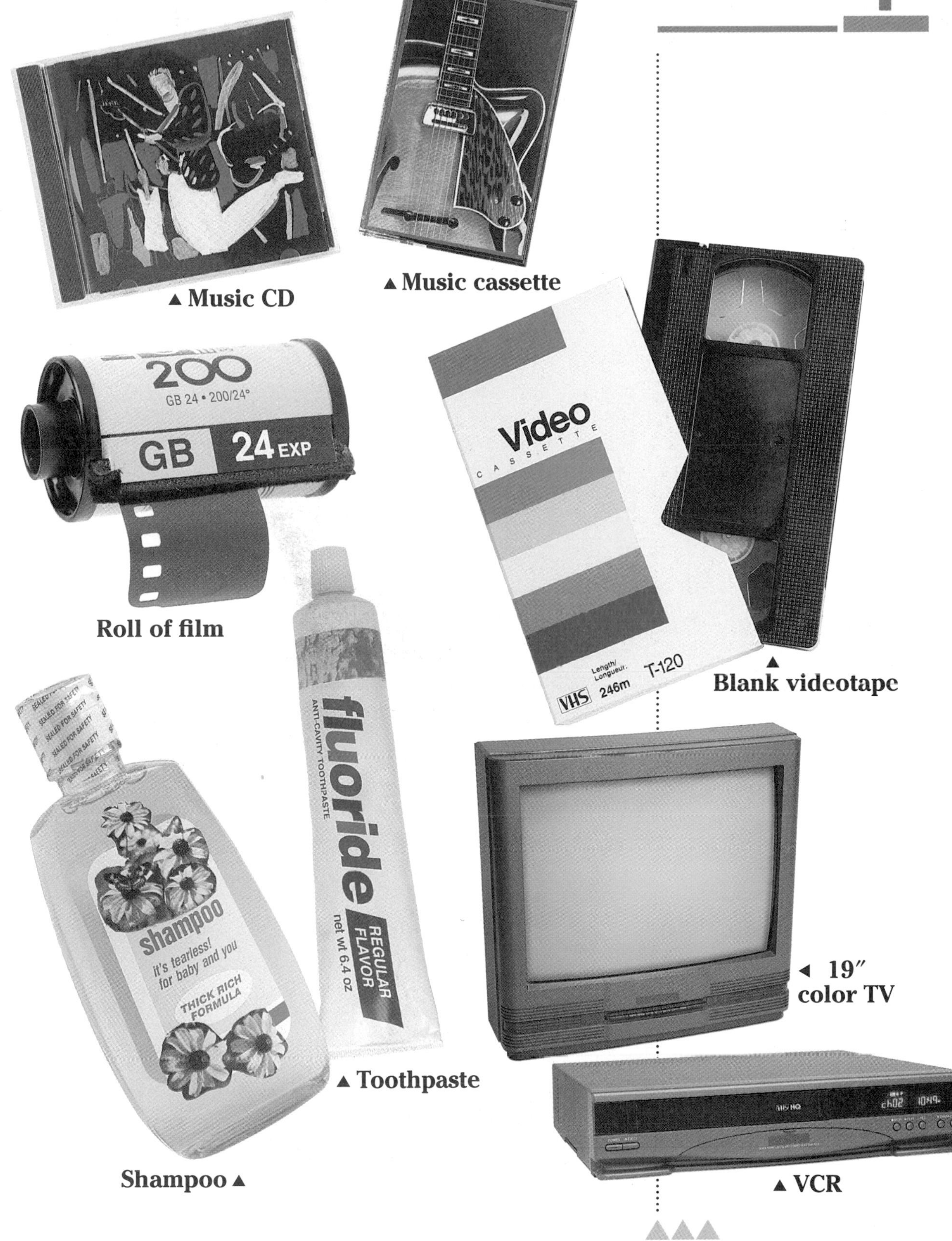

▲ Music CD

▲ Music cassette

Roll of film

▲ Blank videotape

◄ 19″ color TV

▲ Toothpaste

Shampoo ▲

▲ VCR

8. Collect Information

Pairwork. Student A looks at pages 46 and 47 only.
Student B looks at pages 48 and 49 only.

Student A: Ask your partner questions about these items. Write your partner's answers.

Example: *Student A: How much does the basketball cost?*
Student B: *$29.99* .

Student A: Answer your partner's questions about these items.

Example: *Student B: How much does a soccer ball cost?*
Student A: <u>*$24.95*</u>.

$24.95 $129.95 $8.00

$1.99 $7.00 $299.00

Now check your guesses from Activity #7.

Student B: Answer your partner's questions about these items. Write your partner's answers.

Example: *Student A: How much does the basketball cost?*
Student B: <u>*$29.99*</u>.

$29.99

$75.50

$13.00

$2.99

$4.55

$325.00

Student B: Ask your partner about these items.

Example: *Student B: How much does a soccer ball cost?*
Student A: ___*$24.95*___.

Now check your guesses from Activity #7.

9. Compare

Language Focus

A: Which is more expensive, a hot dog or a hamburger?
B: A hamburger.

Classwork. Compare the prices of these foods.

Hot dog \$1.50 Hamburger \$2.75

Which is more expensive, a hot dog or a hamburger?

Pizza \$1.25 Taco \$1.50

Which is more expensive, a slice of pizza or a taco?

Salad \$2.95 Peanut butter sandwich \$1.75

Which is more expensive, a salad or a peanut butter sandwich?

Small soda \$.89

Small glass of milk \$.79

Which is more expensive, a small soda or a small glass of milk?

10. Listen

Classwork. Listen and write the total amount of each order.

A: I'd like a *hamburger and a small soda*, please.
B: That will be $ ________ .

Order	Total Amount
hamburger small soda	
taco small glass of milk	
salad hot dog small soda	
peanut butter sandwich glass of water	

11. Roleplay

Pairwork. Practice ordering from this menu.

MENU

* * *

Hamburger........................$2.70
Hot Dog..............................$1.55
Taco.....................................$1.50
Peanut Butter Sandwich....$1.75
Pizza (1slice)....................$ .99

* * *

Salad..................................$1.95

* * *

Coffee...small..$.75, large....$.90
Soda.....small..$.89, large....$.99
Milk.......small..$.79, large....$.89

Language Focus

A: I'd like ________ .
B: That'll be ________ .
That'll = That will

12. Play a Game

Groupwork. Read the game rules on page 53 and listen to your teacher's instructions.

START →

You lost your wallet. Withdraw $10.00 from your savings account.	You babysat for a neighbor's child. Add $15.00 to your savings account.	You bought a new pair of blue jeans. Withdraw $25.00.
A relative gave you some money. Deposit $10.00.	You lost a library book. Withdraw $20.00.	You bought a new radio. Subtract $30.00.
You went to a movie. Withdraw $7.00.	You need a new pair of sneakers. Withdraw $35.00.	You won a writing contest. Deposit $50.00.
You found some money on the street. Deposit $10.00.	You want to take guitar lessons. Withdraw $60.00.	You bought a present for a friend. Subtract $20.00.
You bought some school supplies—notebooks, pens, etc. Withdraw $10.00.	You painted a neighbor's kitchen. Add $40.00.	You bought a basketball. Subtract $30.00.
You went to the dentist. Withdraw $50.00.	You sold your old bicycle. Deposit $25.00.	You bought a used bicycle. Withdraw $50.00.

BANK

Game Rules

  Take turns tossing two coins.
If you get two heads, move two spaces.

  If you get one head and one tail, move one space.

  If you get two tails, lose a turn. Don't move.

 You can move to the right or left.

 You can move down.

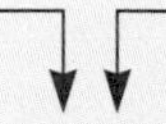 You can move one space to the right or left and then one space down.

You cannot move up.
You cannot move diagonally.  

Start the game with $200.00 in your savings account.
Write your deposits and withdrawals on a chart.
Add or subtract to find the balance.

Example:

Your Bank Savings Account

Date	Deposits (Add)	Withdrawals (Subtract)	Balance
2/15/93	+$200.00		$200.00
2/21/93		-$25.00	$175.00
2/23/93	+$25.00		$200.00

$200.00
-25.00
$175.00

$175.00
+25.00
$200.00

How much money do you have in your bank account at the end of the game?

13. Shared Reading and Writing

What Did People First Use as Money?

Thousands of years ago, people didn't have coins and paper money. They used other things to buy and sell goods. In parts of Africa, Asia, and Australia, people used cowrie shells for money. In Mongolia, people used bricks of tea. In other parts of the world, people used things like salt, beads, cows, stones, fish hooks, and feathers.

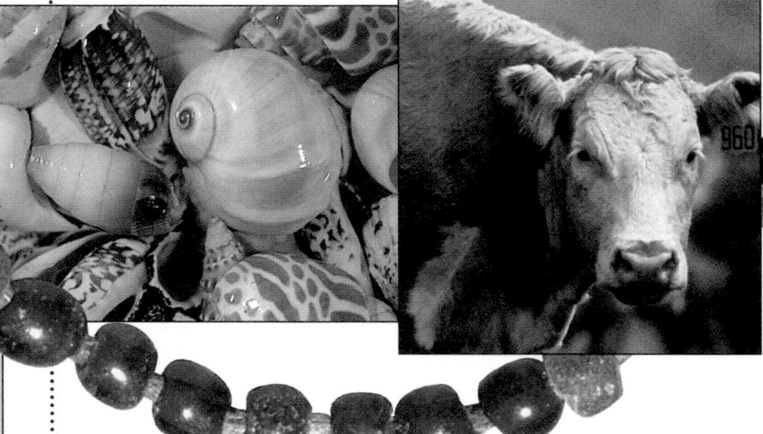

1. Why do you think people started using metal coins and paper money?

2. Besides coins and paper money, what do people use for money today?

14. Match

a. Pairwork. Look at some money from different countries. Complete a chart like this.

What Do You See on the Money?

Country	Words	Numbers	Person	Building	Other
Germany	✔	✔			✔

▲ **Germany**

▲ **People's Republic of China**

▲ **Japan**

▲ **Mexico**

▲ **Malawi**

▲ **Canada**

Language Focus

- I think it's Abraham Lincoln.
- I think Abraham Lincoln is on the penny.

b. Pairwork. Use the information on these pages to answer the questions below.

1. Who is on a penny?
2. Who is on a nickel?
3. Who is on a dime?
4. Who is on a quarter?
5. Who is on a half-dollar?

George Washington
1732–1799
President 1789–1797

George Washington was commander in chief of the Continental Army during the American Revolutionary War (1775–1783). He later became the first president of the United States.

Thomas Jefferson
1743–1826
President 1801–1809

Thomas Jefferson was the third president of the United States. He was also an architect, inventor, lawyer, and writer. He wrote the first draft of the Declaration of Independence.

Abraham Lincoln
1809–1865
President 1861–1865

Abraham Lincoln was the sixteenth president of the United States.
He was president during the American Civil War.

Franklin D. Roosevelt
1882–1945
President 1933–1945

Franklin Roosevelt was the thirty-second president of the United States. He was president during the second World War.

John F. Kennedy
1917–1963
President 1961–1963

John Kennedy was the thirty-fifth president of the United States.

c. Complete a chart like this. Add information about coins from other countries.

Coin	Country	Person on coin
penny	USA	Abraham Lincoln
nickel	USA	
dime	USA	
quarter	USA	
half-dollar	USA	

Language Focus

A: Who's on a Canadian quarter?
B: Queen Elizabeth II.

Activity Menu

Choose one of the following activities to do.

1. Spending Money

Keep a list of your purchases for a week. List everything you buy. Write the price. At the end of a week, find the total.

Day of Week	Purchase	Cost
Monday	lunch notebook	

2. Make a Poster

Make a poster showing the money in your native country. Draw and label the money. Share your poster with the class.

3. Make a Menu

Make a menu with your favorite foods. List the foods and give them a price. Let your classmates practice ordering food from your menu.

4. Plan a Saturday Outing

Plan something special to do on Saturday. Look in the newspaper for ideas. Answer these questions:

- Where will you go?
- How much will it cost?
- How will you get there and back?
- How much will transportation cost?

Report your plan to the class.

5. Dollar Shopping

Visit a store and look for things that cost less than $1.00. How many things can you find? List them. Report what you learned to the class.

6. Collect Money Expressions

Collect expressions about money from several languages and cultures. Report on their meaning.

Example:

"You look like a million bucks." (You look wonderful.)

"A penny for your thoughts." (What are you thinking about?)

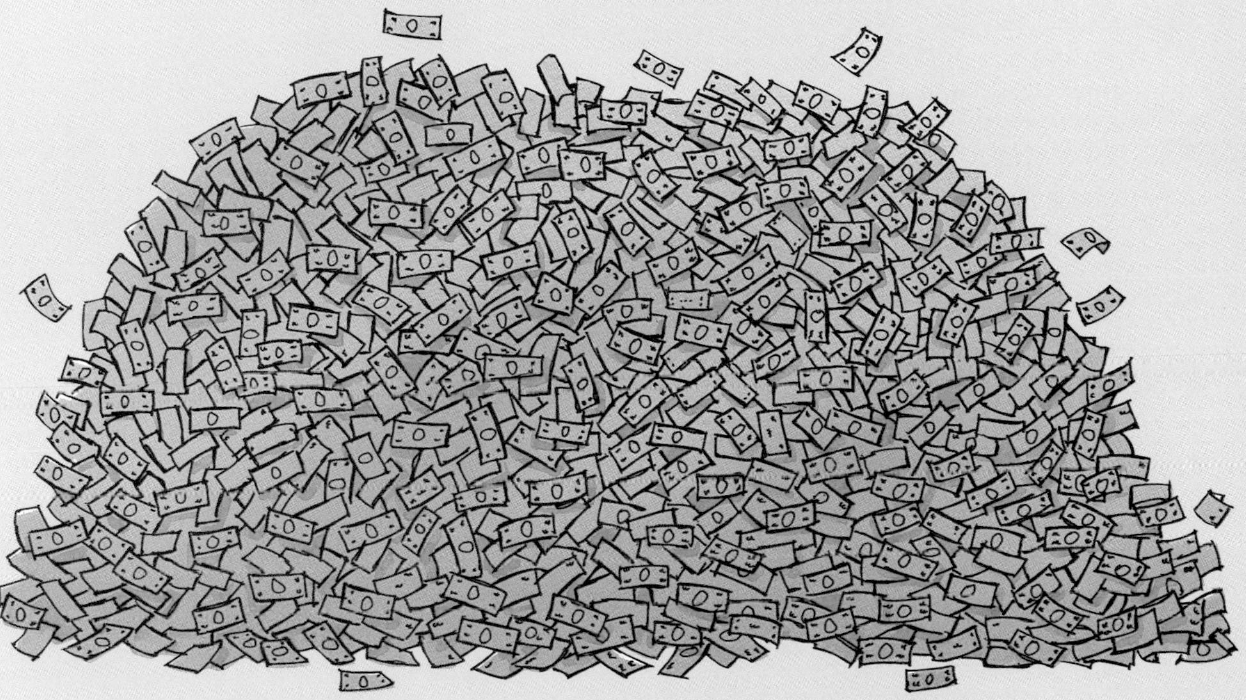

Answers for Activity 6 (page 43)

microscope – $750.00	dictionary – $12.95	notebook – $1.19
computer – $1500.00	eraser – .49	globe – $35.99

Sweater
Woman's Suit
Man's Suit
Socks
Sneakers
Sweatshirt
Shirt
Tie
Baseball cap
Sweatpants
Skirt

Choosing Clothes

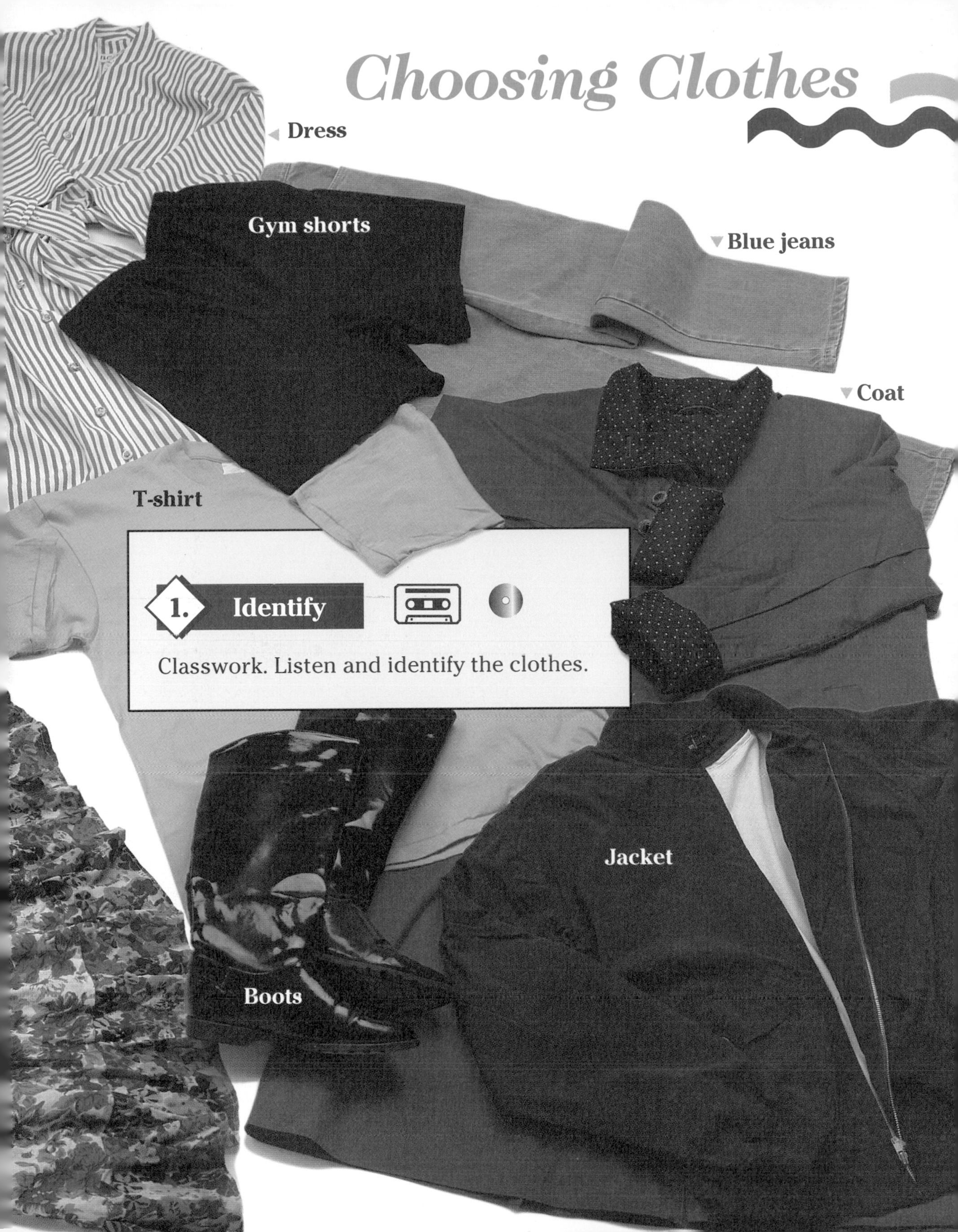

1. Identify

Classwork. Listen and identify the clothes.

2. Describe

Classwork. What are these people wearing?

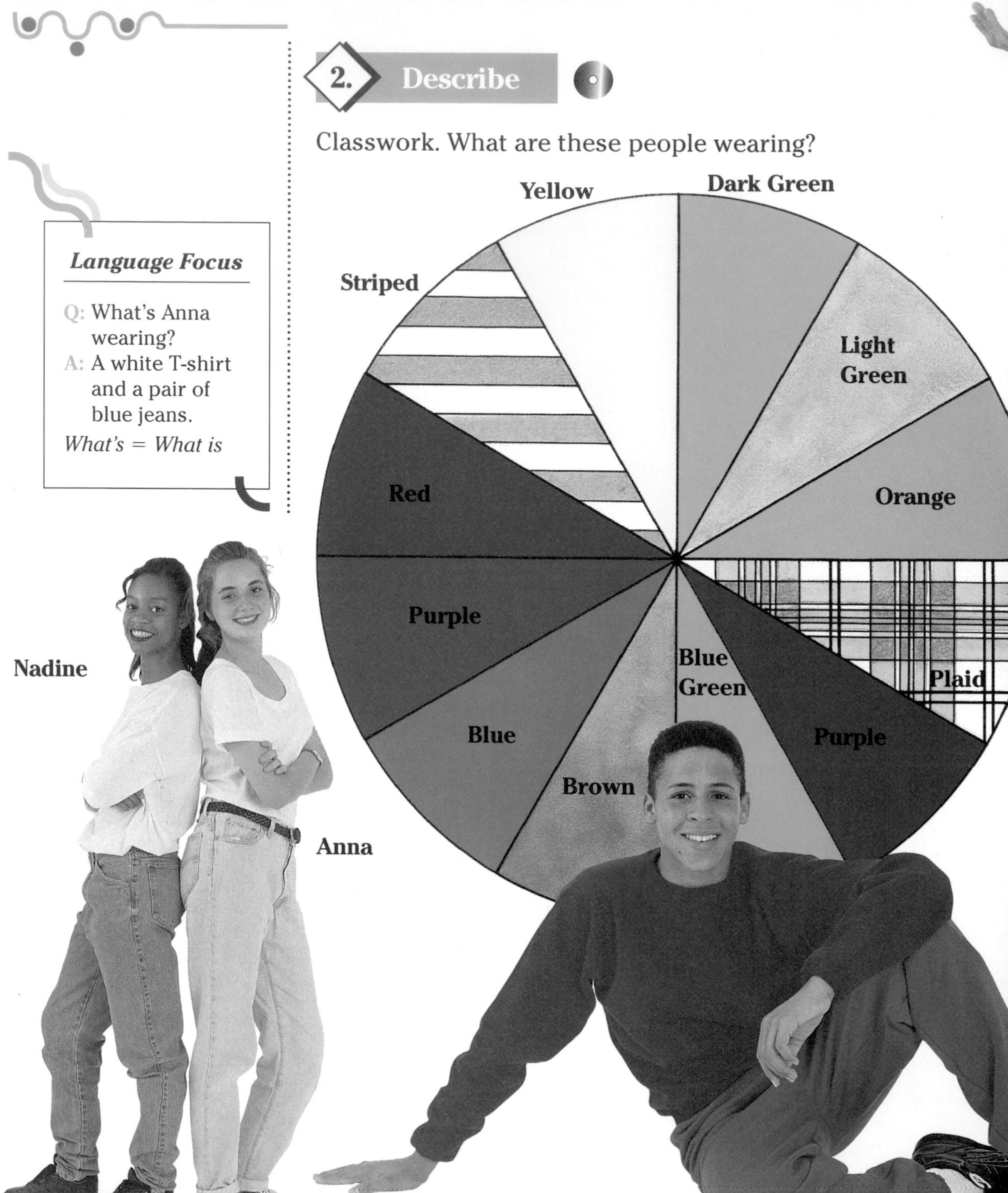

Language Focus

Q: What's Anna wearing?
A: A white T-shirt and a pair of blue jeans.

What's = What is

Marissa
Andy
Karen
Tony

Classwork. Listen to the tape and study the pictures.

What am I wearing?

4. Write

a. On your own. Describe your clothing.

What are you wearing?

I am wearing jeans, a green sweater, and sneakers.

b. Read a classmate's description aloud. Ask your classmates to guess the person.

5. Interview

a. Pairwork. Look at the chart on page 67. Interview a partner. Record your partner's answers in a chart.

Q: Do you like the *red sweater*?
A: Yes, I like it a lot. (It's okay. No, I don't like it at all.)

Q: Do you like the *brown pants*?
A: Yes, I like them a lot. (They're okay. No, I don't like them at all.)

Do you like the . . . ?	a lot +++	okay +	not at all −
red sweater sweatshirt T-shirt ____________			

Language Focus

- I like the red sweater a lot. I like **it** a lot.
- I like the brown pants a lot. I like **them** a lot.

b. Classwork. Listen and write the price for each article of clothing.

Article of clothing	**Price**
red sweater	____________
sweatshirt	____________
__________	____________

c. On your own. Buy an outfit for your partner. Choose clothes your partner likes from the pictures on pages 68–69. Follow the steps below to write a store receipt.

1. List each article of clothing.
2. Write the price for each article of clothing.
3. Add the prices to find the subtotal.
4. To find the tax, multiply the subtotal by .085.
5. To find the total, add the subtotal and the tax.

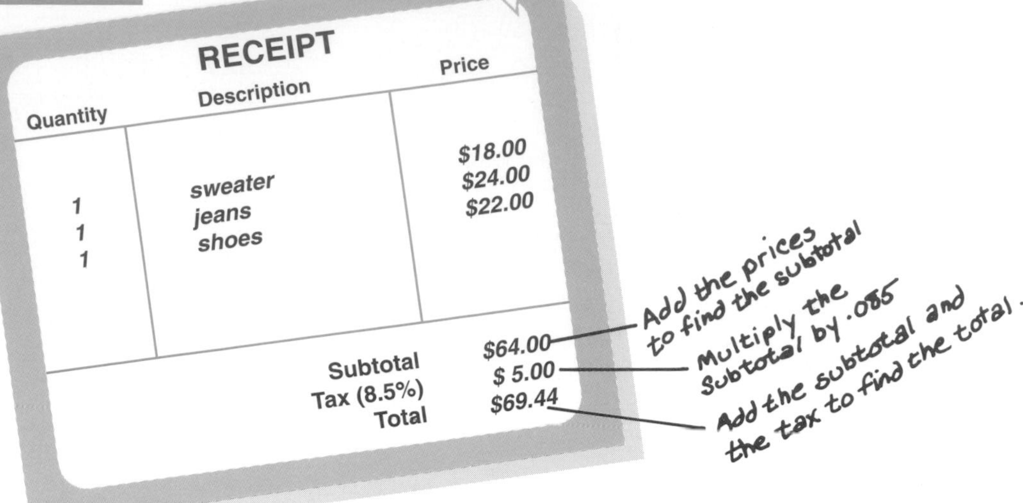

RECEIPT
Quantity
Description
Price
1
1
1
sweater
jeans
shoes
$18.00
$24.00
$22.00
Subtotal
Tax (8.5%)
Total
$64.00
$ 5.00
$69.44
Add the prices to find the subtotal
Multiply the subtotal by .085
Add the subtotal and the tax to find the total.

d. Classwork. Compare receipts. Who spent the most money? Who spent the least money? Who spent the same amount of money?

6. Solve

Groupwork. How much do these clothes cost? Figure out the prices. Then answer the questions below.

Take 50% off

1. Multiply the price by .50.
2. Subtract the result from the price.

Example:
$38.00 × .50 = $19.00
$38.00 − $19.00 = $19.00

Sale Price

brown shoes *$19.00*
black pants ________
leather jacket ________
white sweatshirt ________

Take 20% off

1. Multiply the price by .20.
2. Subtract the result from the price.

Example:
$26.00 × .20 = $5.20
$26.00 – $5.20 = $20.80

Sale Price

black shoes *$20.80*

light brown pants ________

denim jacket ________

blue sweatshirt ________

a. Which pair of shoes is cheaper? *the brown shoes*

b. Which pair of pants is cheaper? ________

c. Which jacket is more expensive? ________

d. Which sweatshirt is more expensive? ________

7. Compare

a. Pairwork. Answer these questions. Record your answers in a chart.

	My Opinion	My Partner's Opinion
1. Which dress is prettier?		
2. Which dress is fancier?		
3. Which pants are baggier?		
4. Which jacket is warmer?		
5. Which women's shoes are more comfortable?		
6. Which skirt is longer?		
7. Which sneakers are nicer?		

b. Pairwork. Practice the dialogue below.

A: Which *skirt* do you like better?

B: The *plaid skirt*.

A: Why?

B: Because *it's prettier*.

c. Pairwork. Tell the class about your partner.

Example: *My partner likes the plaid skirt better.*

Language Focus

- The white dress is prettier.
- The white athletic shoes are more comfortable.

warm → warmer
long → longer
nice → nicer
pretty → prettier
fancy → fancier
baggy → baggier
comfortable → more comfortable

8. Match

Groupwork. These clothes have a special purpose. They protect the body. Match the pictures and the captions.

Surgeons wear face masks to protect themselves from germs.

People wear seat belts to protect their bodies if they have a car accident.

People wear sunglasses to protect their eyes from the sun.

Football players wear helmets to protect their heads.

In cold weather, people wear hats to stay warm.

People wear hats with visors to protect their heads and eyes from the sun.

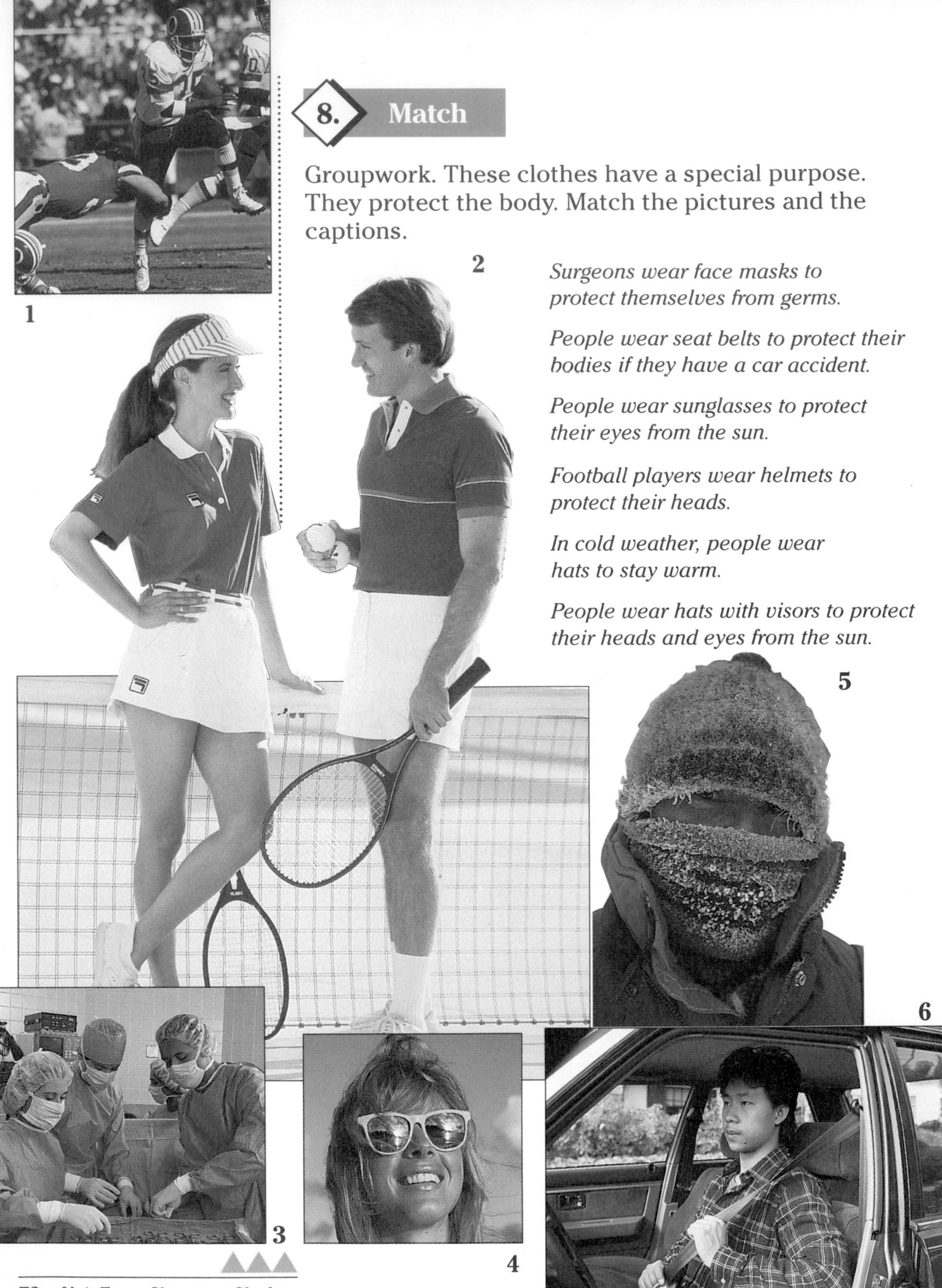

9. Guess

a. Groupwork. What's the purpose of this special clothing? Answer the questions below.

Astronauts wear special clothes when they walk in space.

Language Focus

Q: Why do astronauts wear water-cooled underwear?
A: To stay cool.

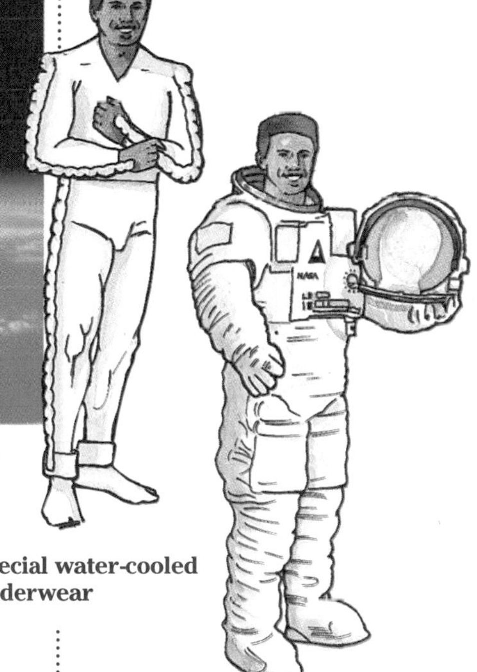

Special water-cooled underwear

Space suit with a computer inside

1. Why do astronauts wear water-cooled underwear?
2. Why do they wear space suits? Why do the space suits have a computer inside?
3. Why do they wear caps with microphones and earphones?
4. Why do they wear bubble helmets? Why do the helmets have a thin layer of gold?

b. Compare your ideas with the answers on page 74.

(Answers)

1. They wear water-cooled underwear to keep cool.
2. They wear space suits to protect their bodies. The space suits provide the right amount of air pressure for their bodies. The computer tells them if the suit is working properly.
3. They wear caps with microphones and earphones to communicate, or talk to each other.
4. The bubble helmets fill with air. This allows the astronauts to breathe. The helmets have a thin layer of gold to protect the astronauts' eyes from the sun.

10. Share Ideas

a. Classwork. Why do you think people wear these clothes? Record your ideas in a chart like this.

	to protect the body	**to be in style**	**because it's a custom**
Why do students in the United States wear black robes at graduation?			✓
Why do some people wear neckties?			
Why do some women wear high-heeled shoes?			
Why do some people in the desert wear loose robes?			
Why do workers on a ranch wear boots?			
In some countries, brides wear white dresses. In some countries, they wear red dresses. Why?			

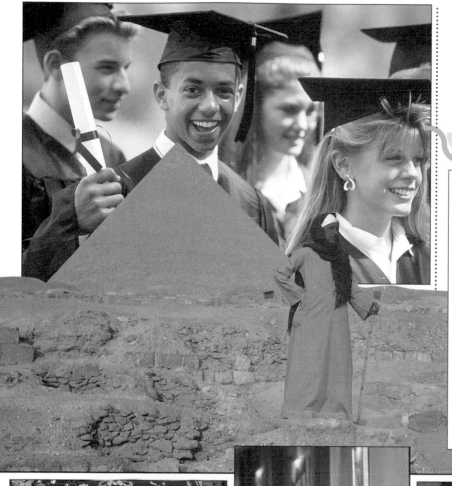

Language Focus

Q: Why do students in the United States wear black robes at graduation?
A: Because it's a custom.
Q: Why do some women wear high-heeled shoes?
A: To be in style.

b. Groupwork. Add your ideas to a chart like this.

What do people wear to protect their bodies?	What do people wear to be in style?	What do people wear because it's a custom?
gloves		*kimonos (Japan)*

11. Plan

a. Groupwork. Take a trip. Choose one of these places to visit for a week.

A ranch in Texas

The island of Hawaii

The mountains in Maine

b. What are you going to do there? Brainstorm a set of ideas.

things to do

Language Focus

- We're going to swim.
- We're going to ride bikes.

c. Choose ten articles of clothing to take in your suitcase.
Example: *I'm going to take a jacket.*

d. Exchange lists with another group. Which place are they going to visit? Make a guess.

12. Write

a. On your own. Follow the steps below.

1. Find or draw a picture of an interesting outfit.
2. Label all the parts.
3. Where are you going to wear this outfit? Write your answer on a card like this.

> *I'm going to wear this outfit to*
> ______________________________.

b. Classwork. Mix up everyone's cards and pictures. Then try to match them.

Language Focus

- I'm going to wear this outfit to go on a picnic.
- I'm going to wear this outfit to play basketball.

13. Shared Reading

a. Classwork. Study the shoes in the picture on the next page. Choose words to describe the shoes.

These words are opposites.

cheap	↔	expensive
soft	↔	stiff
clean	↔	dirty
comfortable	↔	uncomfortable
old	↔	new

Language Focus

- I think they are expensive.
- They look expensive.

b. Classwork. Read this poem aloud with your classmates.

Ode to My Shoes

My shoes from America,
they are very expensive and soft.
They help me to walk.
When I go somewhere,
they go with me, too.
They come to school with me.
When I go back home,
my shoes stay under my bed.
Sometimes they look very happy.
When they are torn,
they look like they are smiling.
When they are dirty,
they look very sleepy.
I like my shoes.

—Harjit Singh (former student, Newcomer High School)

What's an Ode?

An ode is a poem that praises something. It tells why the poet likes something.

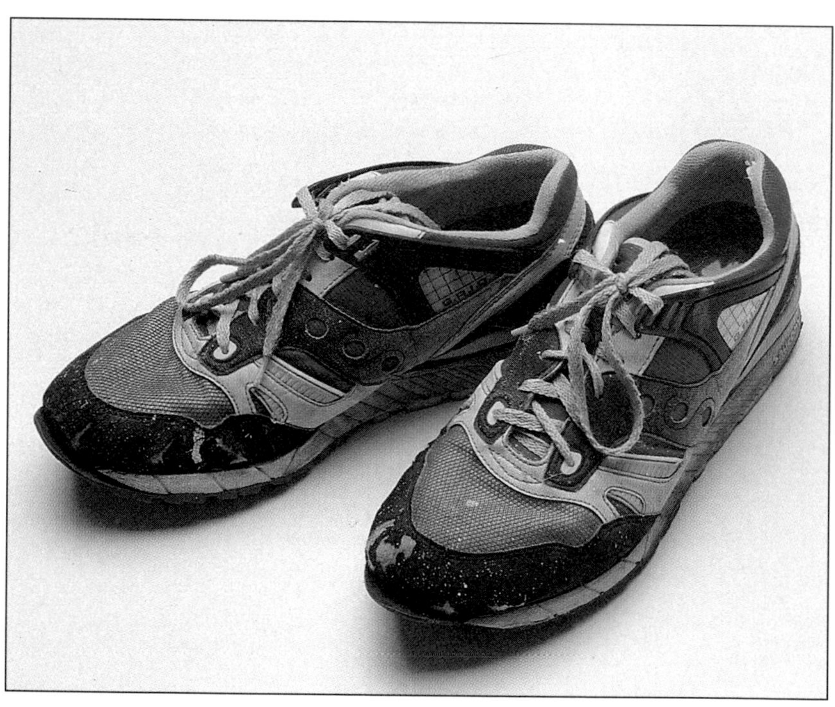

14. Write

a. On your own. What's your favorite clothing?

My favorite clothing is *a pair of blue sweatpants*.

b. List words to describe your favorite clothing.

blue, old, holey, comfortable

c. Quickwrite about your favorite clothing. Try to write without stopping for three minutes. Here are some questions you might think about as you write:

1. What does this clothing look like?
2. Where do you like to wear this clothing?
3. How do you feel when you wear this clothing?

Example:

My favorite clothing is a pair of blue
sweatpants. They are very old and they
have lots of holes. But they are very
comfortable. I feel energetic when I wear
them. At night I hang them over a chair.
Then they look tired. I only wear them
at home because they are so old. My
mother wants to throw them out but
I wont let her...

c. Use the ideas in your quickwriting to write an ode to your favorite clothing.

Activity Menu

Choose one of the following activities to do.

1. School Dress Code
The school dress code tells what you can and can't wear at school. What is the dress code at your school? Copy and illustrate the rules, and post them in your classroom.

2. Spend $100 on Clothes
Imagine that you have $100 to spend on new clothes. Look through a catalog of clothing, and make your choices. Fill out an order form, and show it to your classmates. Make sure you don't spend more than $100.

3. Clothing Around the World
Study pictures of people in a different country. Tell your classmates about the clothing in this country.

4. Clothing Advice
What do people in your native country wear at this time of year? Tell your classmates what clothes to take on a trip to your native country.

5. Collect Pictures
Collect pictures of people in different professions. Group the people by profession. Describe their clothing, and tell your classmates what people wear to work in different professions.

6. Clothing for Special Occasions
Write about a ceremony in which people wear special clothing. Describe the clothing and the occasion. Share your writing with your classmates.

7. Taking Care of Clothes

Read the labels on several items of clothing. Find out from what kinds of fabric they are made. Read the cleaning or washing instructions. Write the information in a chart. Show your chart to the class.

Kind of fabric	Instructions
100% Acrylic	Machine wash cold Tumble dry low Do not bleach

8. Make a Pie Graph

Choose an article of clothing made from different kinds of fabrics. Make a pie graph showing the percentage of each fabric.

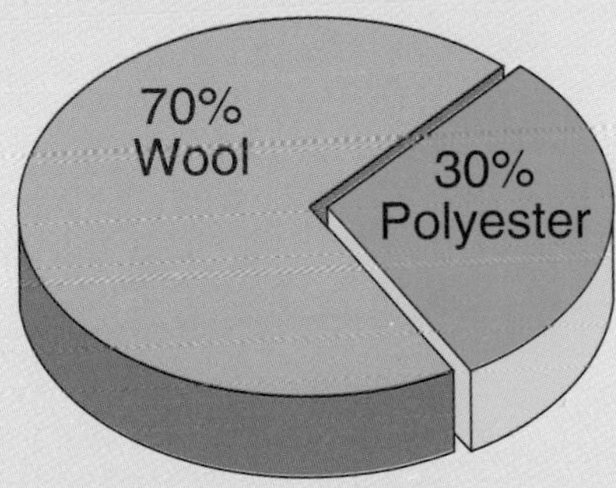

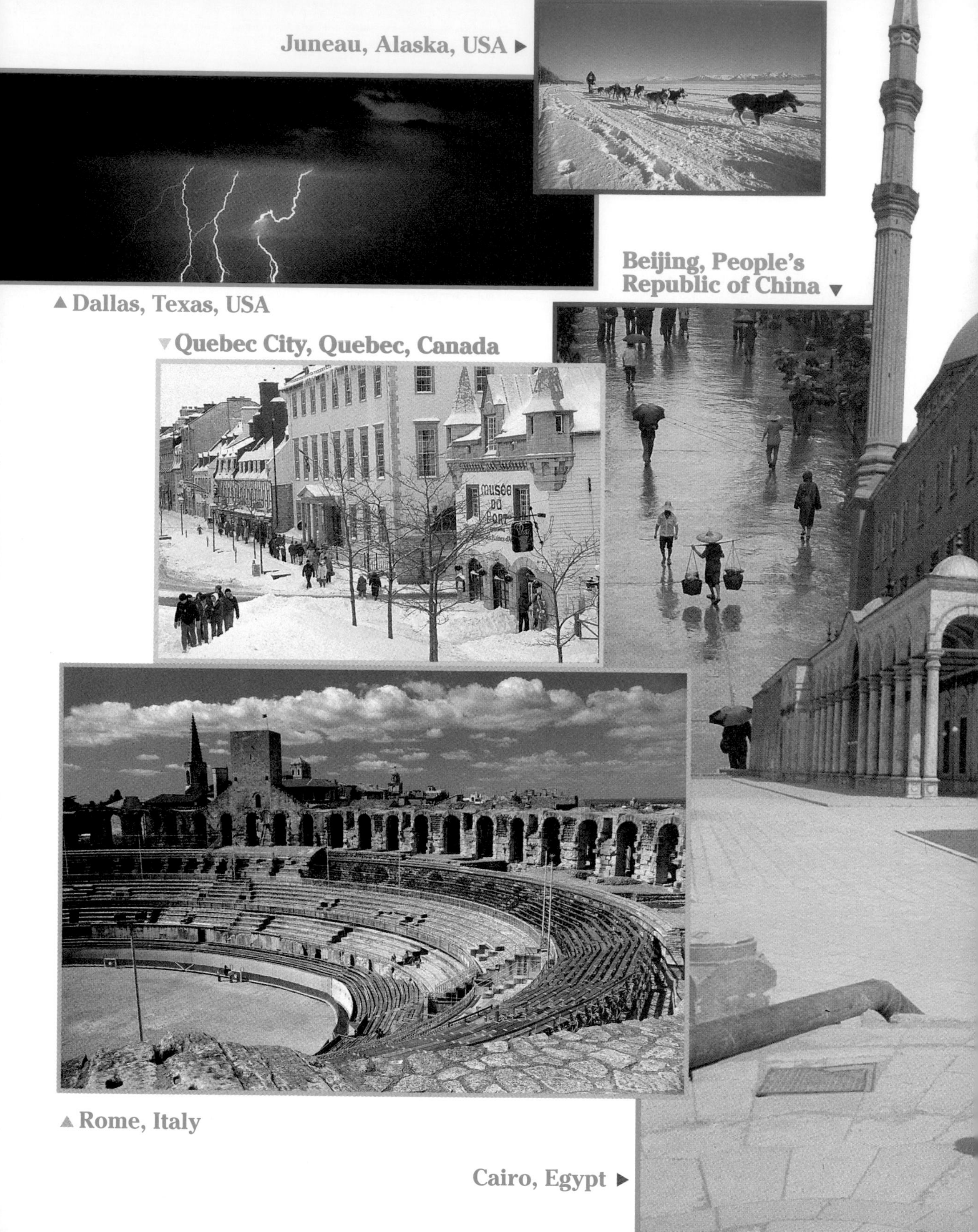

Juneau, Alaska, USA ▶

▲ Dallas, Texas, USA

Beijing, People's Republic of China ▼

▼ Quebec City, Quebec, Canada

▲ Rome, Italy

Cairo, Egypt ▶

Checking the Weather

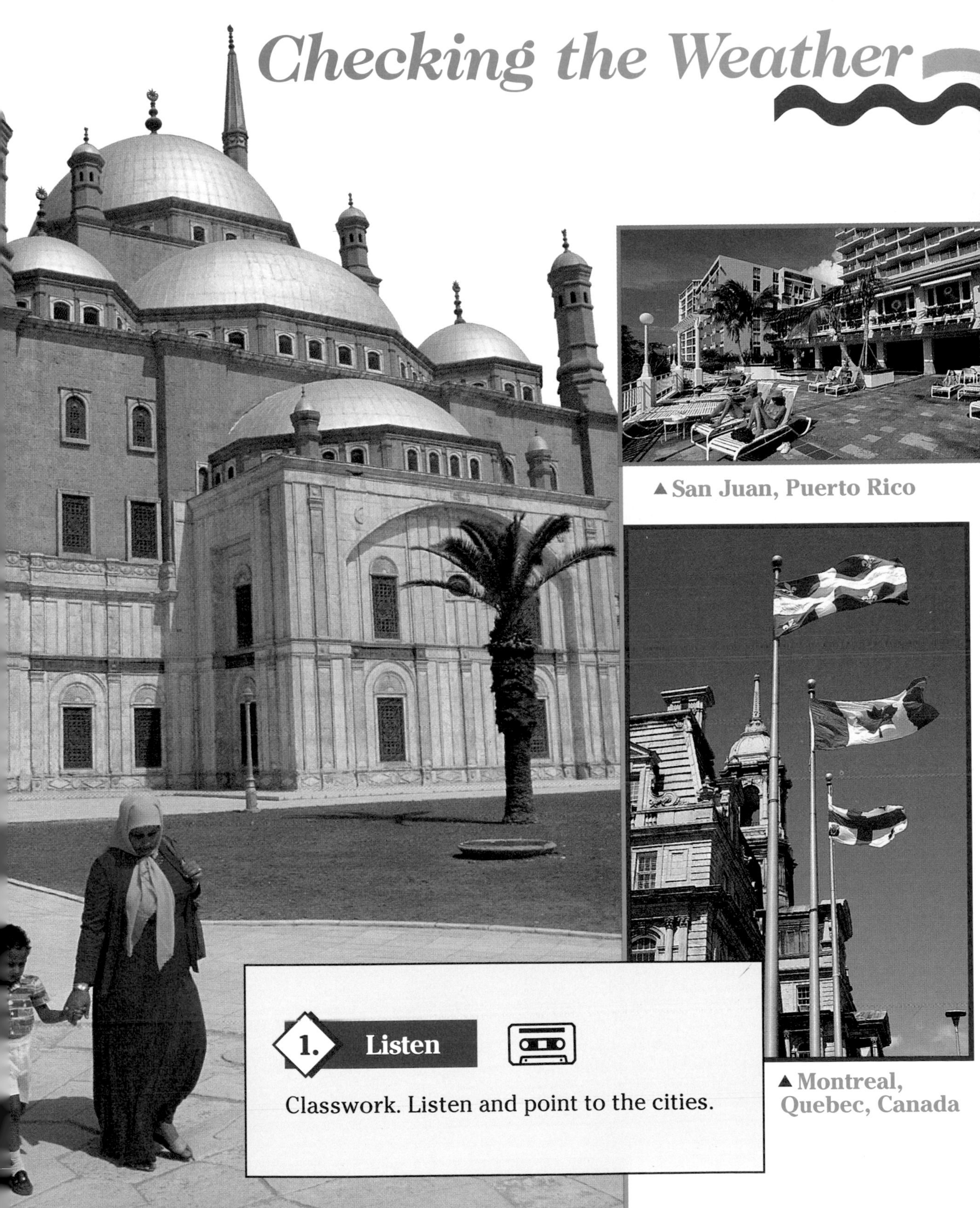

▲ San Juan, Puerto Rico

▲ Montreal, Quebec, Canada

1. Listen

Classwork. Listen and point to the cities.

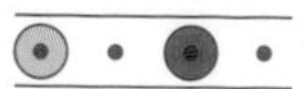

2. Identify

a. Classwork. Listen and identify these cities.

Boston, Massachusetts, USA
Chicago, Illinois, USA
Toronto, Ontario, Canada
Mexico City, Mexico
Portland, Maine, USA
Vancouver, British Columbia, Canada

4

b. On your own. Write about the weather in your area today.

Language Focus

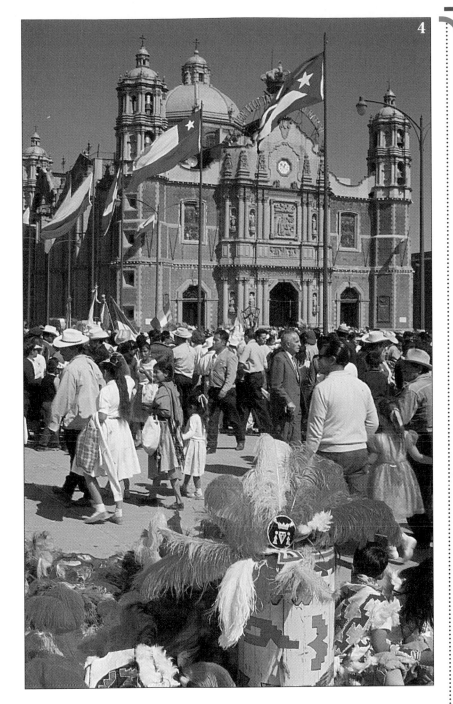

It's raining in Boston.

It's raining.	It's sunny.
It's snowing.	It's cloudy.
It's storming.	It's windy.
	It's cold.
	It's cool.
	It's warm.
	It's hot.

3. Read Symbols

a. Pairwork. Choose a place on the weather map. Describe tomorrow's weather.

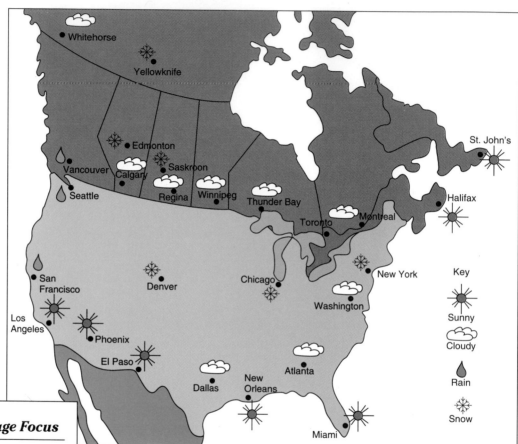

Language Focus

- It's going to be sunny in Miami tomorrow.
- It's going to be cloudy in Calgary tomorrow.
- It's going to rain in Seattle.
- It's going to snow in Yellowknife.

b. Pairwork. Find two places with the same weather symbols. Describe the weather.

Example: *It's going to be sunny in Miami and El Paso.*

4. Listen

a. Classwork. What are they going to do tomorrow? Listen and complete a chart.

	Dialogue #1	Dialogue #2
What's the weather going to be like?	______	______
What are they going to do tomorrow?	______	______

b. Pairwork. Read a weather forecast for your area. Then practice this dialogue.

A: What do you want to do tomorrow?

B: I don't know. I think it's going to *be sunny*.

A: Then let's *do something outdoors*.

B: Okay.

c. On your own. Answer these questions.

1. What are you going to do tomorrow if it rains?
   If it rains tomorrow, I am going to ______.

2. What are you going to do tomorrow if it's sunny?
   If it's sunny tomorrow, I ______.

5. Describe

Classwork. Tell about the weather in your area.

Yesterday	Today	Tomorrow
Date: *October 24* *It rained.* *It was cold.*	Date: *October 25* *It's raining.* *It's cold.*	Date: *October 26* *It's going to rain.* *It's going to be cold.*

Language Focus

Yesterday it *was cloudy.*
. . . *rained*
. . . *snowed*
. . . *was sunny*
. . . *was windy*

6. Analyze

a. Classwork. Read the thermometers on the next page. What was the temperature in each city on February 23?

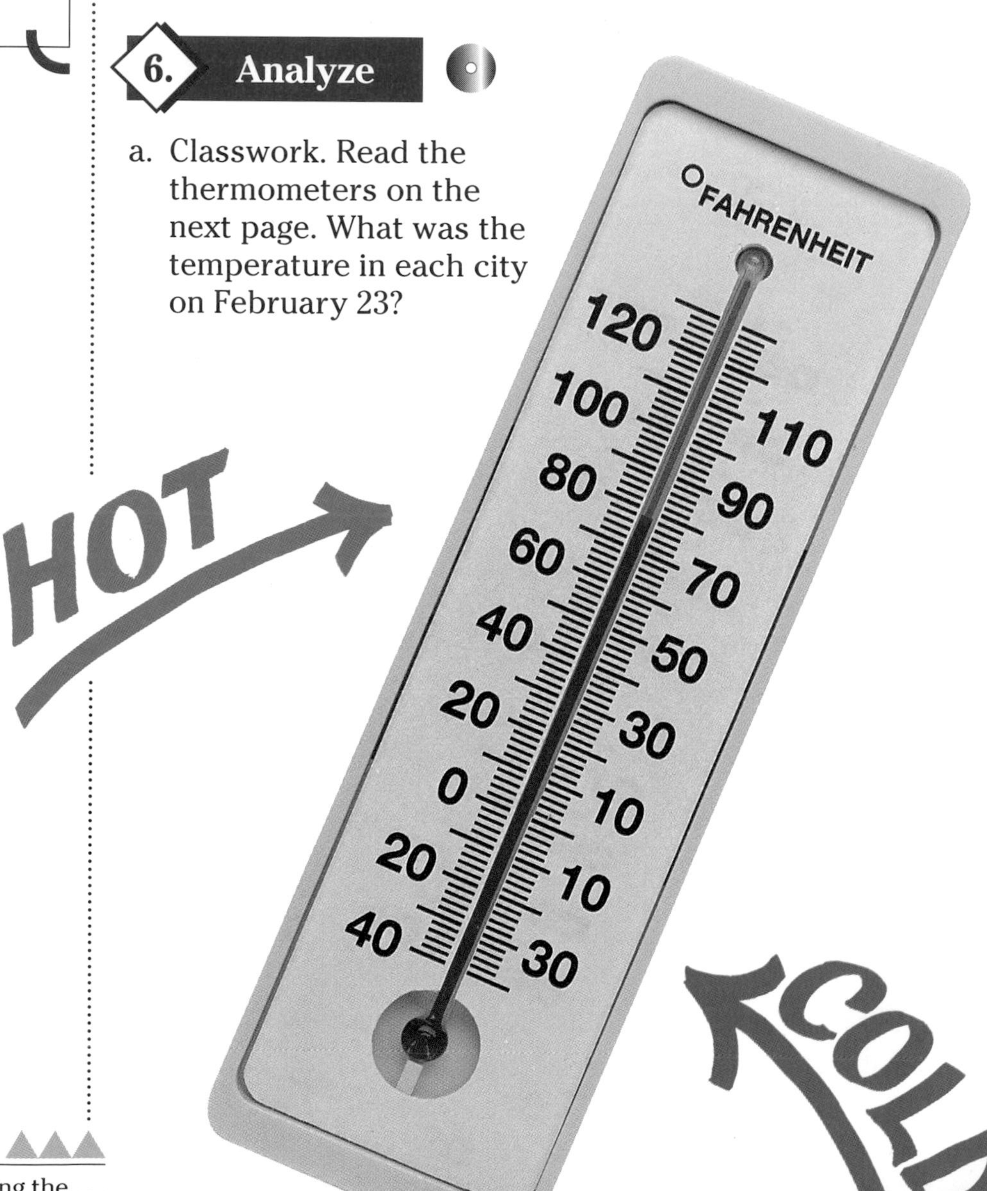

Dallas, Texas

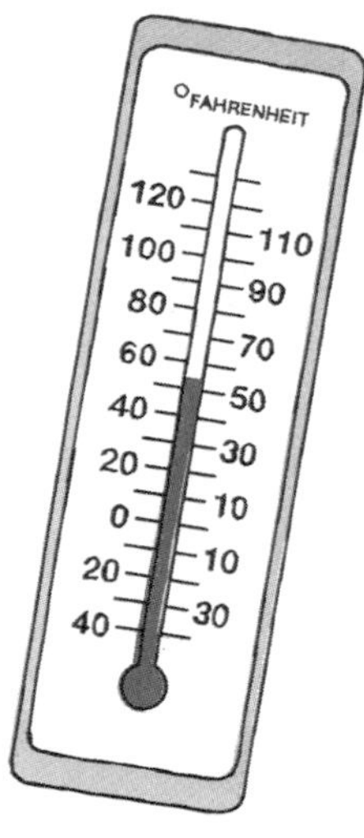

Seattle, Washington

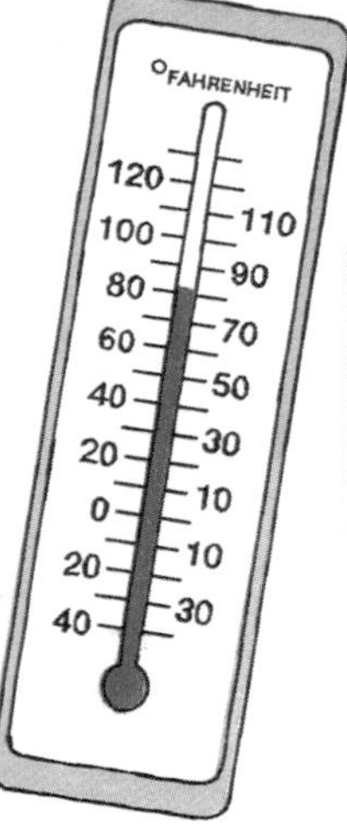

Miami, Florida

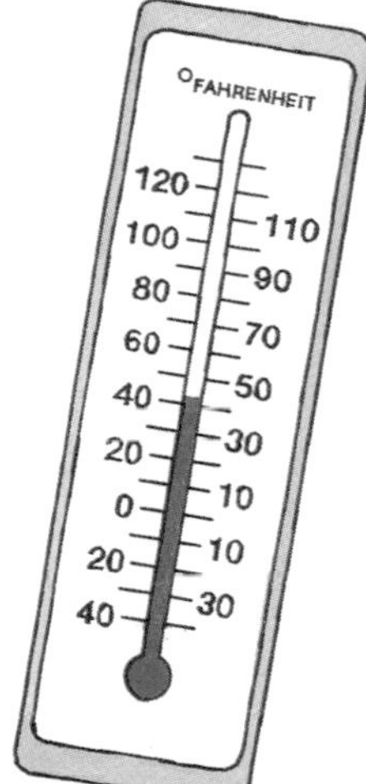

Chicago, Illinois

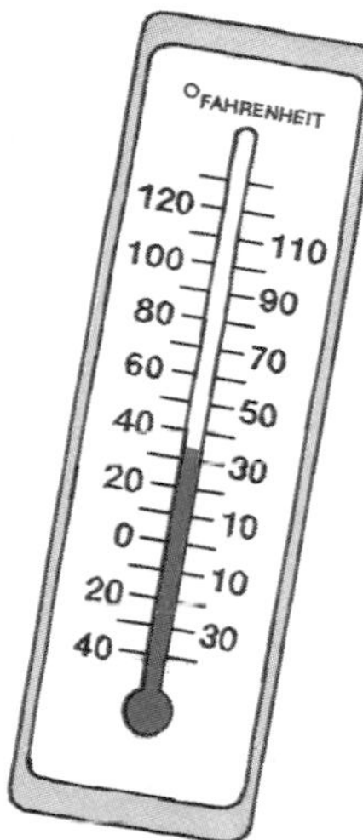

Toronto, Ontario

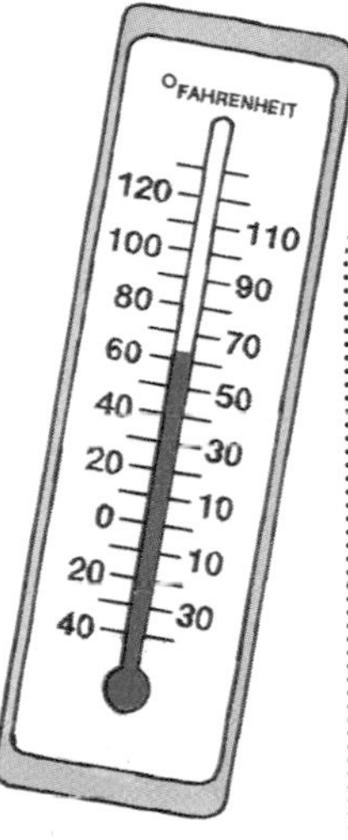

New Orleans, Louisiana

b. Pairwork. Take turns asking and answering questions.

Q: Was it hotter in Dallas or Seattle?

A: It was hotter in ______________________.

Q: Was it colder in Toronto or New Orleans?

A: ______________________.

Q: ______________________?

A: ______________________.

Language Focus

- It was 75° Fahrenheit in Dallas, Texas.
- It was 54° Fahrenheit in Seattle, Washington.

7. Solve

a. Classwork. Was it hotter in Los Angeles, California, or Rio de Janeiro, Brazil? Follow these steps to find out:

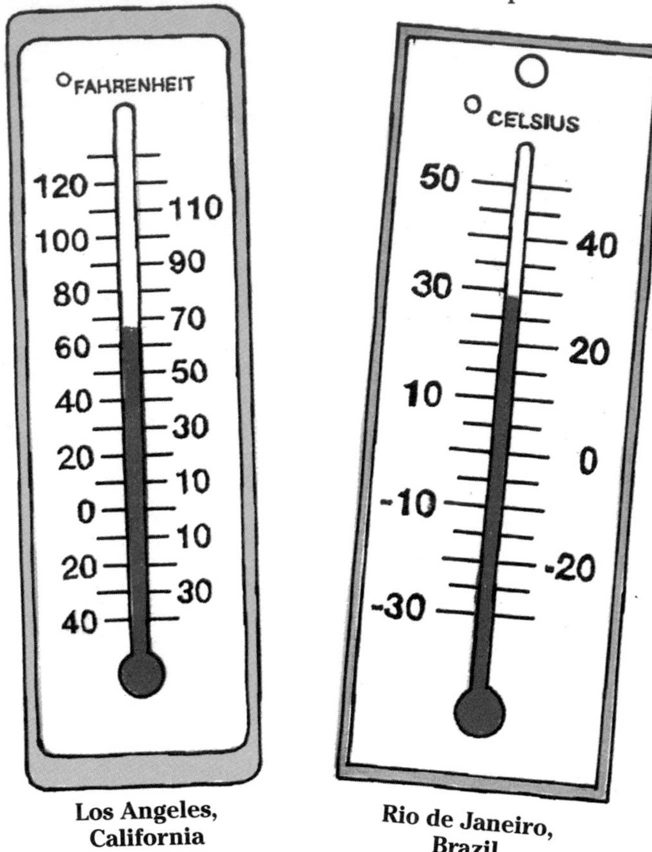

Temperature on February 23

Measuring Air Temperature

In most countries in the world, people use the Celsius (*Centigrade*) scale to measure air temperature.

In the United States, people use the *Fahrenheit* scale to measure air temperature.

0° Celsius = 32° Fahrenheit.

Steps:

1. Convert the temperature of Rio de Janeiro to Fahrenheit.

> *To convert Celsius to Fahrenheit*
> a. Multiply the temperature by 9.
> b. Divide by 5.
> c. Add 32.

2. Compare the temperatures in Rio de Janeiro and Los Angeles.

3. Check your answer. Convert the temperature of Los Angeles to Celsius.

> *To convert Fahrenheit to Celsius*
> a. Subtract 32 from the temperature.
> b. Multiply by 5.
> c. Divide by 9.

4. Compare the temperatures in Los Angeles and Rio de Janeiro.

b. Groupwork. Put these cities in order from the hottest to the coldest.

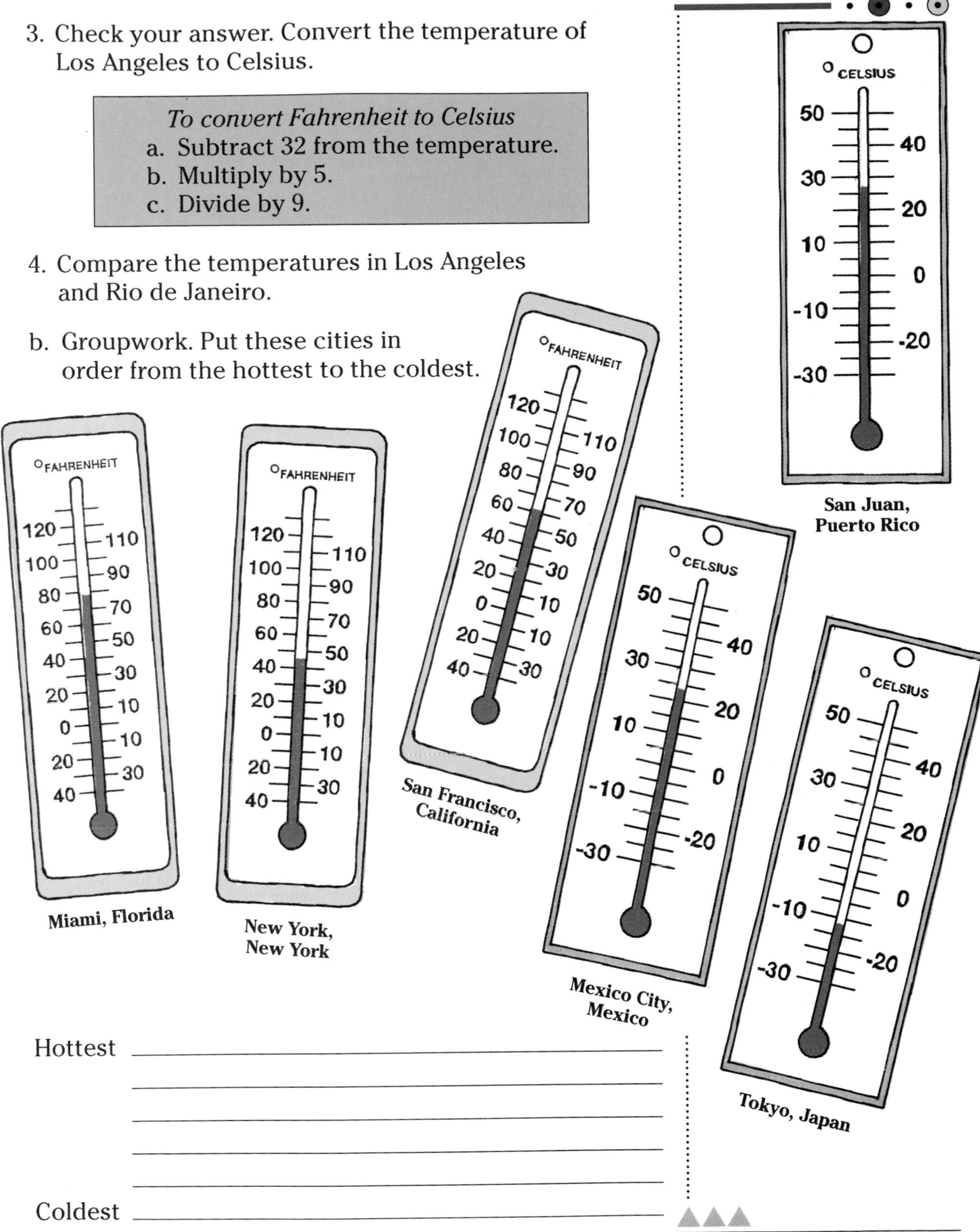

Hottest ______________________________

____

____

____

____

Coldest ______________________________

8. Find the Average

Groupwork. Follow the steps below to find the average temperature for the day.

These thermometers measured the temperatures in Los Angeles and New York at different times during one day.

1 A.M.

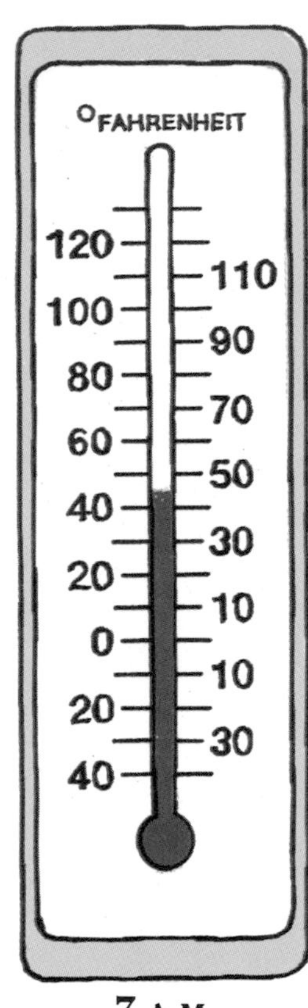

7 A.M.

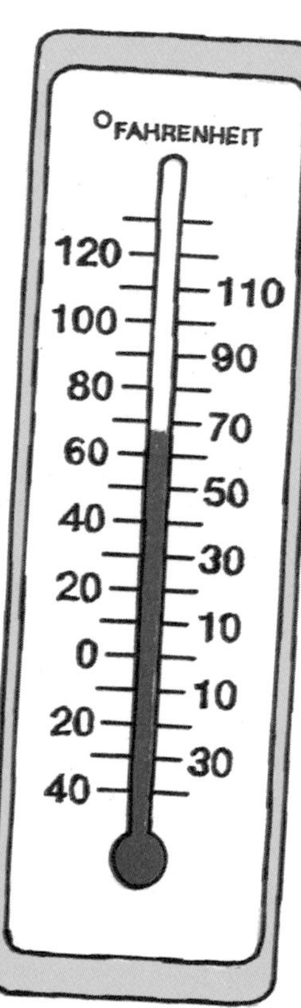

1 P.M.

7 P.M.

Los Angeles
California

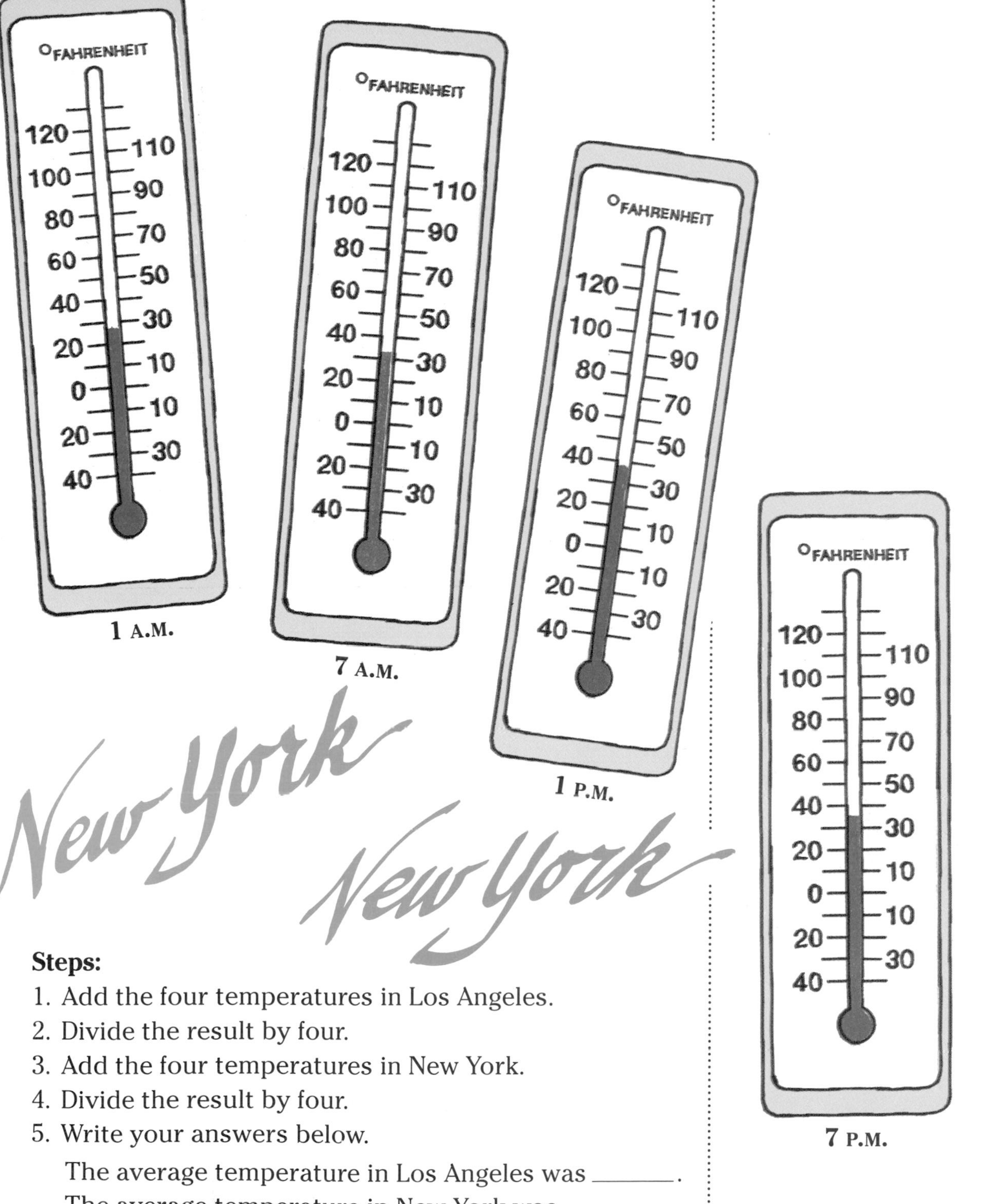

Steps:

1. Add the four temperatures in Los Angeles.
2. Divide the result by four.
3. Add the four temperatures in New York.
4. Divide the result by four.
5. Write your answers below.

The average temperature in Los Angeles was ______.

The average temperature in New York was ______.

9. Read a Chart

Classwork. Compare the temperatures in Los Angeles and New York.

This chart shows the average monthly temperatures in Los Angeles and New York.*

City	January	April	July	October
Los Angeles	56	59.5	69	66.3
New York	31.8	51.9	76.4	57.5

*temperatures in degrees Fahrenheit

In January
In April
In July
In October

the average monthly temperature was higher
the average monthly temperature was lower

in Los Angeles
in New York

Would you rather live in Los Angeles or New York? Why?

10. Read a Graph

Classwork. Use the chart above to complete a line graph.

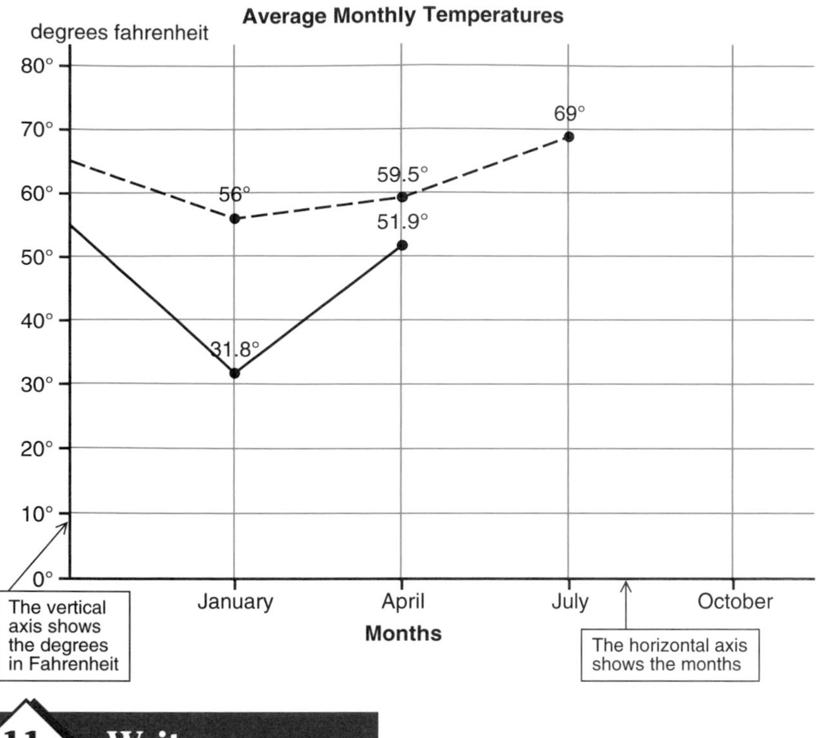

New York
Los Angeles

11. Write

Pairwork. Compare the average monthly temperatures in Boston, Massachusetts, and Seattle, Washington. Write several sentences.

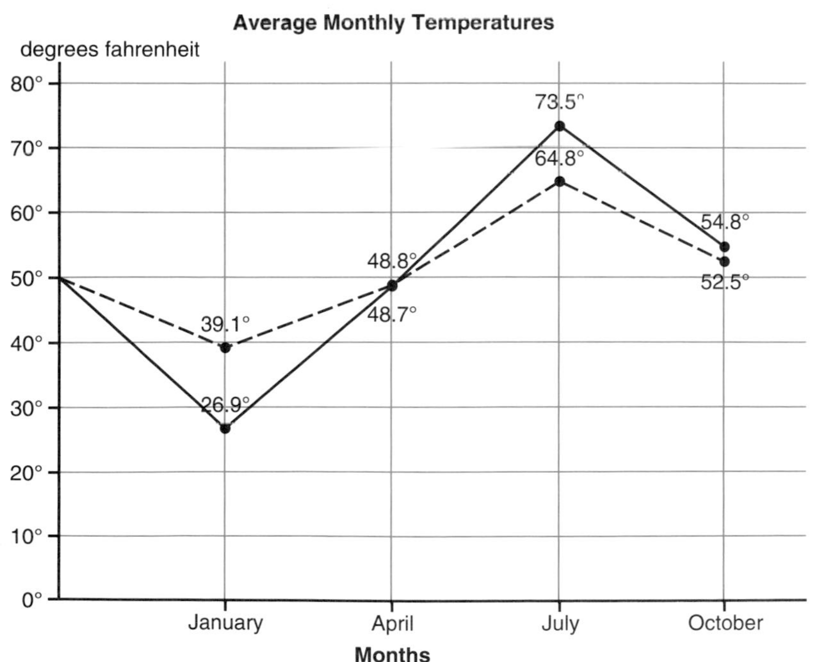

Language Focus

- In January, it was warmer in Seattle.
- In April, it was colder in Boston.

Boston, Massachusetts
Seattle, Washington

12. Make a Line Graph

a. Pairwork. Imagine a city. Give it a name. What do you want the weather to be like? Choose the average monthly temperatures. Write them in a chart.

*This chart gives the average monthly temperatures**
in __________________________ .
(name of your imaginary city)

City	January	April	July	October

*temperatures in degrees Fahrenheit

b. Groupwork. Add your average monthly temperatures to a class line graph. Then compare temperatures in your ideal cities.

13. Investigate

a. Pairwork. On a hot day, do you feel cooler in dark-colored clothes or light-colored clothes? Choose a or b.

Our prediction:

a. You feel cooler in light-colored clothes.

b. You feel cooler in dark-colored clothes.

b. Classwork. Test your prediction. Try this investigation on a sunny day:

Materials: two room or outdoor thermometers, sheets of black paper and white paper of the same size and thickness

Steps:

1. Find a room with a sunny window. Measure the air temperature in the room.
2. Put the thermometers in a sunny place.
3. Cover one thermometer with white paper. Cover the other thermometer with black paper. Leave them for 30 minutes.
4. Remove the paper. Read the temperature. Record your data.

1.
2.

3.
4.

Color of Paper	Temperature at the beginning	Temperature after 30 minutes
Black		
White		

c. Pairwork. Was your prediction correct?

14. Match

a. Classwork. Find these places on the map on pages 104–105.

- Antarctica
- Ethiopia, Africa
- Sahara Desert, Africa
- United States, North America
- Chile, South America

b. Groupwork. Guess the answers to these questions. Choose places from the list above.

1. Where is the hottest place on earth?
2. Where is the coldest place on earth?.
3. Where is the windiest place on earth?
4. Where is the sunniest place on earth?
5. Where is the wettest place?
6. Where is the driest place?

c. Compare answers with your classmates.

d. Check the facts on page 99.

Language Focus

The hottest place on earth is ______ .
The coldest place is ______ .

Answers:

1. *Hottest place (average over a year)—Dallol, Ethiopia (34.4 degrees C)*
2. *Coldest place (average over a year)—Vostok, Antarctica (−257.8 degrees C)*
3. *Windiest place—George V Coast, Antarctica (320 kph winds)*
4. *Sunniest place—Sahara, Africa (−4300 hours a year)*
5. *Wettest place—Mt. Waialeale, Hawaii (11,684 mm a year)*
6. *Driest place—Atacama Desert, Chile*

15. Predict

Classwork. Read this information and make a prediction.

In the story below, the wind and sun argue about something. Study the pictures and tell what you think they argue about.

Maybe they argue about ....

16. Reader's Theater

Classwork. Listen to the story.

The North Wind and the Sun

NARRATOR: One day, the north wind and the sun got into an argument.

NORTH WIND: I'm stronger than you.

SUN: Impossible! I'm much stronger than you.

NORTH WIND: Never! I am stronger.

NARRATOR: Just then, the north wind saw a traveler walking on the road below.

NORTH WIND: Let's test our strength on that traveler. I'm sure I can make her take off her coat faster than you can.

SUN: Impossible. I'm certain to win.

NARRATOR: The north wind tried first. He blew down hard on the traveler. He blew harder and harder, but the traveler held onto her coat.

SUN: Now it's my turn.

NARRATOR: At first, the sun shone gently on the traveler, who soon unbuttoned her coat. Then the sun shone in full strength. Before long, the traveler took off her coat and continued her journey without it.

17. Share ideas

Classwork. Share ideas about the story with your classmates. Here are some questions to think about.

1. What was the argument about?
2. The wind and the sun showed their strength in different ways. How?
3. This Reader's Theater is based on a fable—a story that teaches a lesson. What lesson do you think this fable is trying to teach?

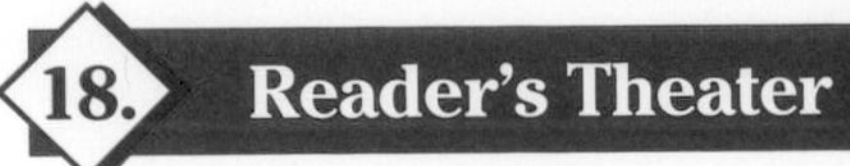

18. Reader's Theater

Groupwork. Make a story map.

Title: The North Wind and the Sun

Problem

What was the problem?
The wind said he was stronger.
The sun said she was stronger.

Plot (What happened?)

What did they decide to do?
They decided to ______________
____

What did the North Wind do? *He blew hard on the traveler.*	**What did the Sun do?** ______________ ______________
What happened? ______________ ______________	**What happened?** ______________ ______________

19. Roleplay

Groupwork. Get together in groups of three. Practice reading the story "The North Wind and the Sun." Then act it out for your classmates.

Activity Menu

Choose one of the following activities to do.

1. What's the weather?
Collect pictures (photographs or copies of paintings) that show different kinds of weather. Write captions for the pictures and display them.

2. Be a Weather Forecaster
Watch a TV weather forecaster. What props does the forecaster use? What information does this person give? Use what you learn to make a weather forecast to your classmates.

3. Collect Weather Songs
Think of a song about the weather. Write down the words in English or another language. Read the words to your classmates. Tell them what the song means.

4. Stay Cool
Wearing light-colored clothing can help you to stay cool. What are some other ways to stay cool in hot weather? And how can you stay warm in cold weather? Make a chart listing ways to stay cool and keep warm. Present your suggestions to the class.

5. Keep a Weather Journal
Record each day's weather in a notebook. Draw columns for the date, temperature, and weather conditions.

6. Graph the Temperature in Your Area
Look in an almanac for the average monthly temperatures of U.S. cities. (Look in the index under *Temperatures.*) Choose a city in your area and make a line graph of the temperatures. Each month, compare the actual temperature to the average temperature on your graph.

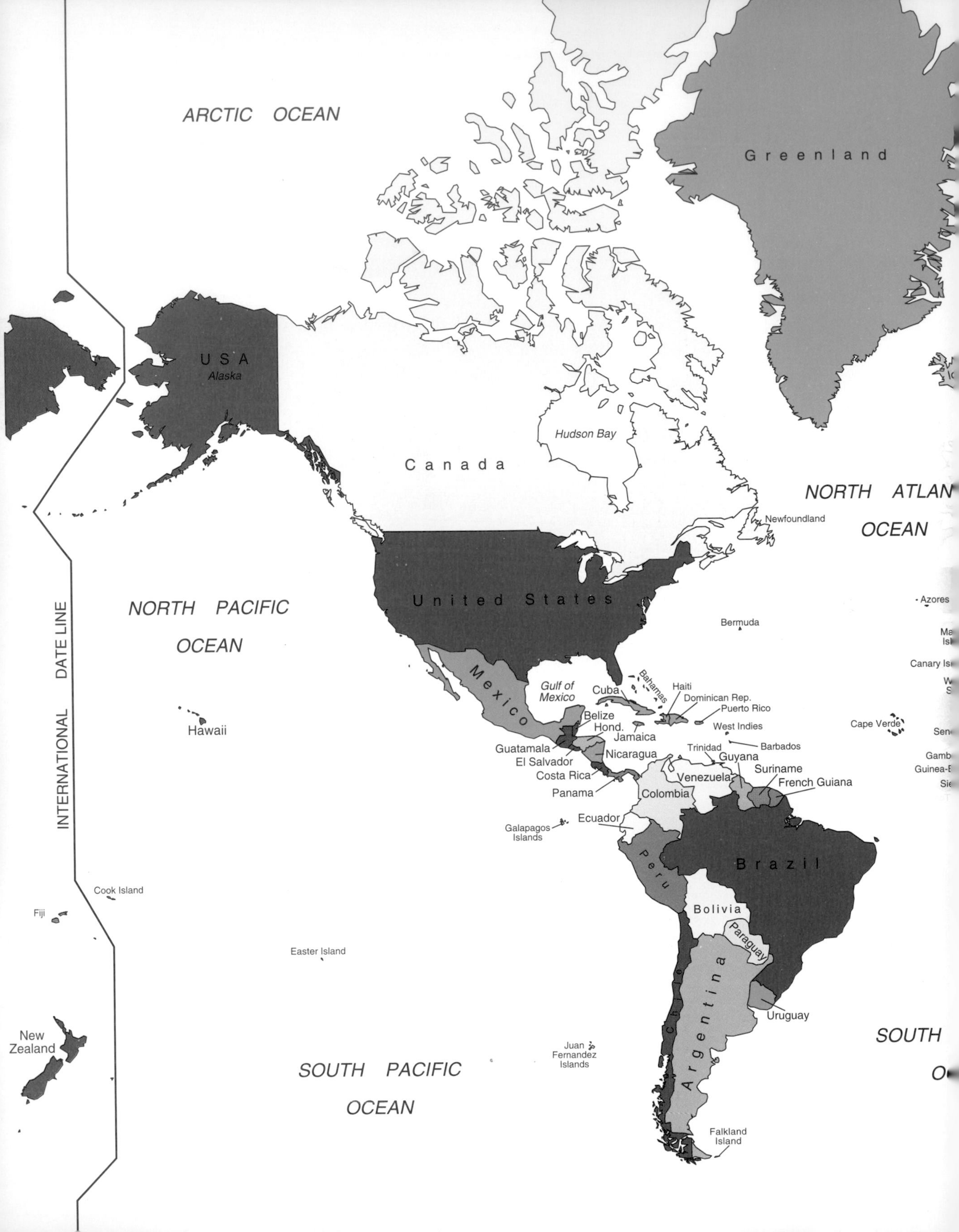

ARCTIC OCEAN
Greenland
USA
Alaska
Hudson Bay
Canada
NORTH ATLAN
OCEAN
Newfoundland
United States
NORTH PACIFIC
OCEAN
INTERNATIONAL DATE LINE
Azores
Bermuda
Canary Is
Mexico
Gulf of Mexico
Cuba
Bahamas
Haiti
Dominican Rep.
Puerto Rico
West Indies
Cape Verde
Hawaii
Belize
Hond.
Jamaica
Guatamala
El Salvador
Costa Rica
Panama
Nicaragua
Trinidad
Barbados
Guyana
Suriname
French Guiana
Venezuela
Colombia
Ecuador
Galapagos Islands
Peru
Brazil
Bolivia
Paraguay
Chile
Argentina
Uruguay
Cook Island
Fiji
Easter Island
New Zealand
Juan Fernandez Islands
SOUTH PACIFIC
OCEAN
SOUTH
Falkland Island

Making Journeys

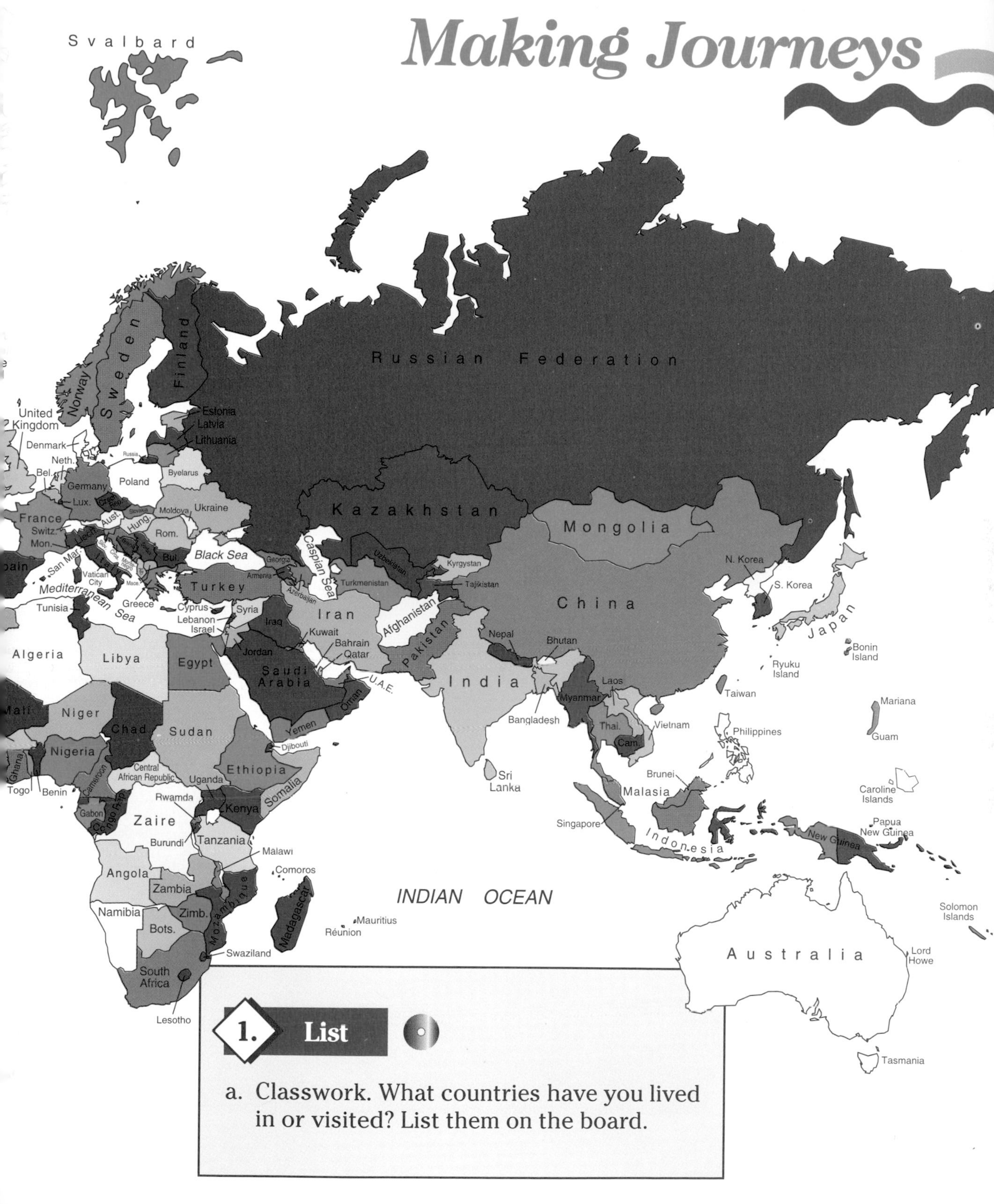

1. List

a. Classwork. What countries have you lived in or visited? List them on the board.

b. Classwork. Group the countries on your list.

Continents of the World

Africa	Antarctica	Asia	Australia	Europe	North America	South America
Zaire		*Laos*			*Canada*	

Which continents has no one in the class visited?

Language Focus

- Canada is in North America.
- Laos is in Asia.
- Zaire is in Africa.

a. Classwork. Answer the questions on page 107.

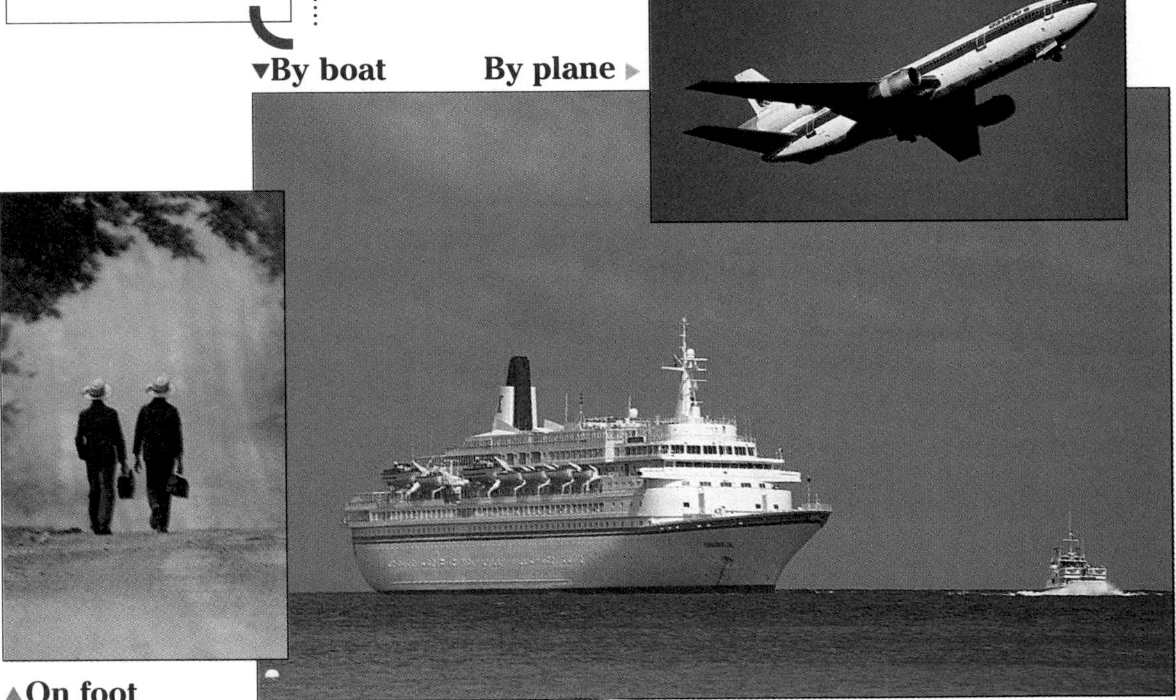

▼By boat

By plane ▶

▲On foot

How can you get from . . . ?	by car	by boat	by plane	on foot
Italy to Brazil		✓	✓	
Canada to Mexico				
People's Republic of China to Turkey				
Saudi Arabia to Afghanistan				
Puerto Rico to Bolivia				
________ to ________				

Language Focus

- You can get from Italy to Brazil by boat.
- You can't get from Italy to Brazil by car.

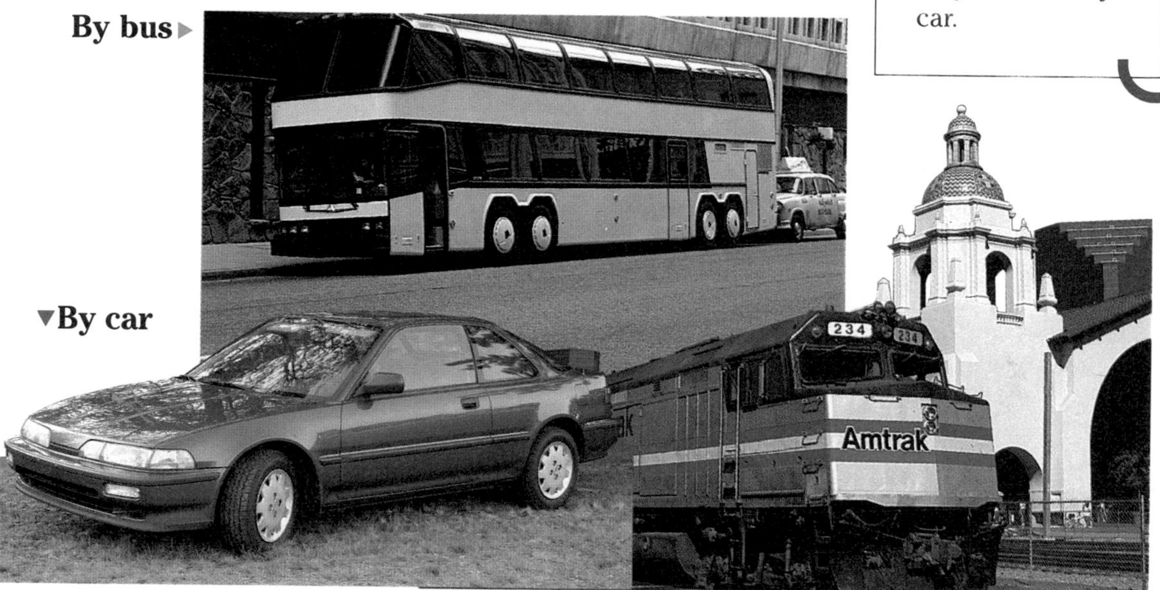

By bus

By car

By train

b. Groupwork. Write three questions. Then read your questions to another group.

Can you get from ______ to ______ by ______ ?

c. Groupwork. Add the names of countries to this chant. Then read your chant to the class.

Getting There

You can get from ______ to ______ by boat,
but you can't get there by ______.
You can get from ______ to ______ by car,
but you can't get there by ______.
You can get from ______ to ______ by plane,
but you can't get there by boat.

Language Focus

Q: Can you get from India to Korea by boat?
A: Yes, you can.
Q: Can you get from Australia to Mexico by car?
A: No, you can't.

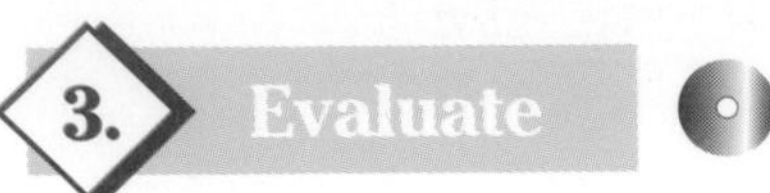

3. Evaluate

a. Groupwork. Answer these questions. Tell what you think.

What is . . . ?	
the fastest way to travel	*by plane*
the slowest way to travel	
the most expensive way to travel	
the least expensive way to travel	
the safest way to travel	
the most dangerous way to travel	
the most comfortable way to travel	
the least comfortable way to travel	

b. Report your group's answers to the class.

Example:
The fastest way to travel is *by plane*.

c. Pairwork. Think about a trip you took. Then take turns asking and answering the questions below.

Example: Q: When did you take this trip?
A: *Last year*.
Q: Where did you go?
A: *To New York*.
Q: How did you get there?
A: *By bus*.

d. Write a sentence about your partner's trip. Then read the sentence to the class.

Example:
Last year, my partner went to New York by bus.

Language Focus

Q: What is *the fastest* way to travel?
A: By plane.

the fastest
the slowest
the safest
the most expensive
the most comfortable
the most dangerous
the least expensive
the least comfortable

4. Preview

Classwork. Study the pictures on pages 110-112. How can you travel across the continent of Antarctica? Share ideas with your classmates.

You can travel	You can't travel
on foot	*by car*

Language Focus

- You can travel on foot.
- You can't travel by car.

5. Describe

a. Classwork. Look again at the pictures on pages 110-112. Then choose the words below that describe Antarctica.

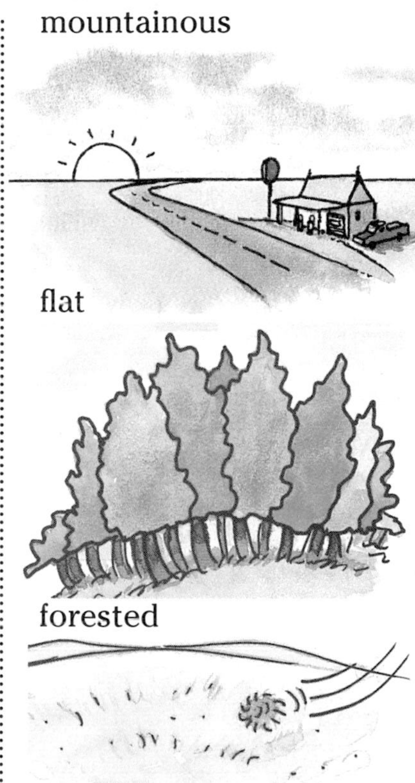

b. Classwork. Add information about Antarctica to a diagram like this. Use words from the list on page 108 and your own ideas.

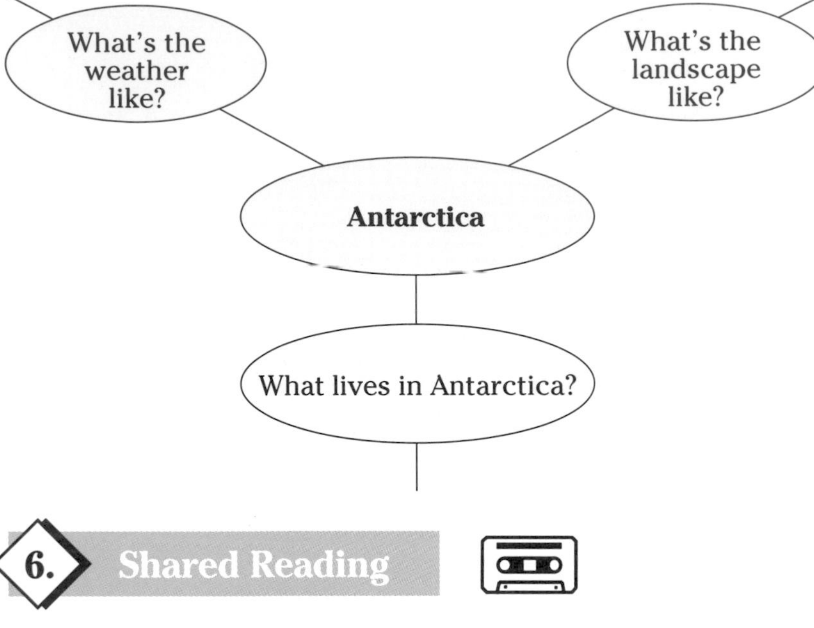
What's the weather like?
What's the landscape like?
Antarctica
What lives in Antarctica?

6. Shared Reading

Read about Antarctica and add more ideas to your diagram.

Crossing Antarctica

Antarctica, the land of the South Pole, is the world's coldest, iciest, and windiest continent. Scientists have recorded a temperature of minus 128.6°F (−89.2°C) in Antarctica! Ice more than a mile thick covers 98 percent of the land. Along the coast, scientists have recorded winds of up to 200 miles (322 kilometers) an hour.

Almost no life can exist in the interior of Antarctica. Along its shores and in the surrounding waters, however, a variety of wildlife lives. Penguins, seals, whales, and many kinds of fish swim in the ocean surrounding Antarctica.

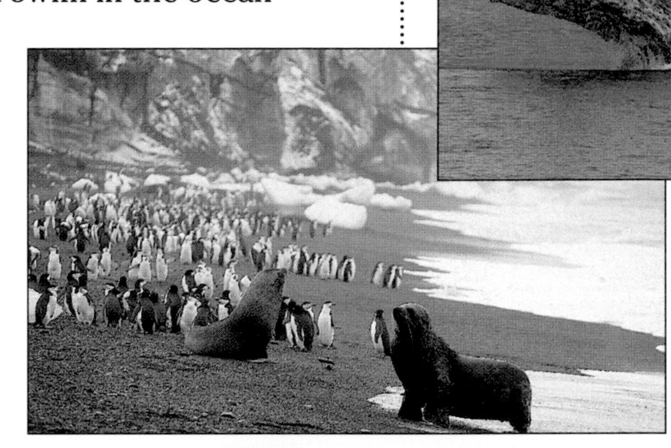

In 1989, a six-person team spent 221 days traveling across the continent of Antarctica. The team included scientists and explorers from the former Soviet Union, China, Japan, France, Britain, and the United States. They traveled across the continent on cross-country skis while 36 dogs pulled their equipment.

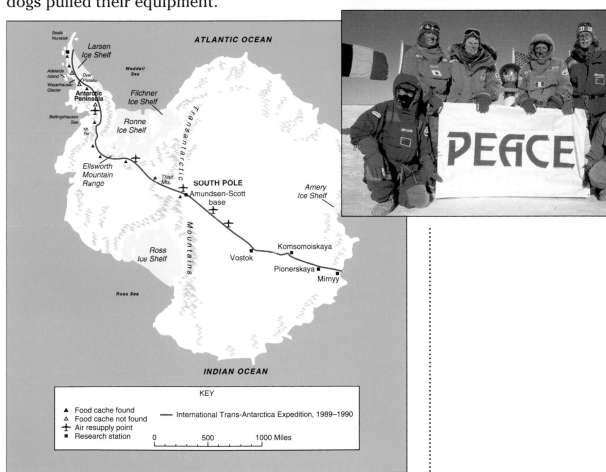

Seals Nunatak
Larsen Ice Shelf
ATLANTIC OCEAN
Weddell Sea
Adelaide Island
Dyer Plateau
Weyerhauser Glacier
Antarctic Peninsula
Filchner Ice Shelf
Bellingshausen Sea
Mt. Re
Ronne Ice Shelf
Transantarctic Mountains
Ellsworth Mountain Range
Thiel Mts.
SOUTH POLE
Amundsen-Scott base
Amery Ice Shelf
Komsomoiskaya
Ross Ice Shelf
Vostok
Pionerskaya
Mirnyy
Ross Sea
INDIAN OCEAN

KEY

▲ Food cache found
△ Food cache not found
Air resupply point
■ Research station
International Trans-Antarctica Expedition, 1989–1990
0 500 1000 Miles

The team traveled an average of 17 miles a day. Sometimes, the traveling was difficult and dangerous. Strong winds and snow made it difficult to see and the explorers worried about getting lost. They also had to cross an area with crevasses in the ice. Many times, the dogs fell into these deep holes and the explorers had to pull them out.

"It's really like another planet," said one team member. "The weather is always trying to kill you. It's typically 30 degrees below zero with winds of 30 miles per hour. That's a common day."

7. Analyze

a. On your own. Tell if you agree or disagree with the statements below.

1. It's colder in North America than in Antarctica.
2. Ice covers much of Antarctica.
3. There aren't any animals in Antarctica.
4. Traveling across Antarctica is dangerous.
5. You can travel across Antarctica by car.
6. A crevasse is a deep hole.

b. Compare ideas with your classmates.

8. Evaluate

a. Groupwork. The explorers took the items below on their trip across Antarctica. Put these items into two groups.

Necessities (things you need to stay alive in Antarctica)	**Luxuries** (things you don't need to stay alive)
food	*camera*

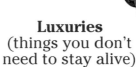

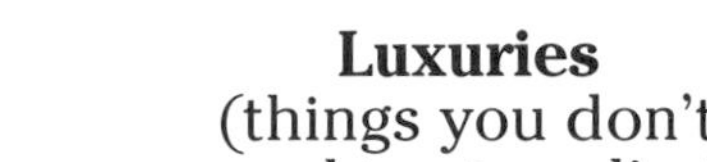

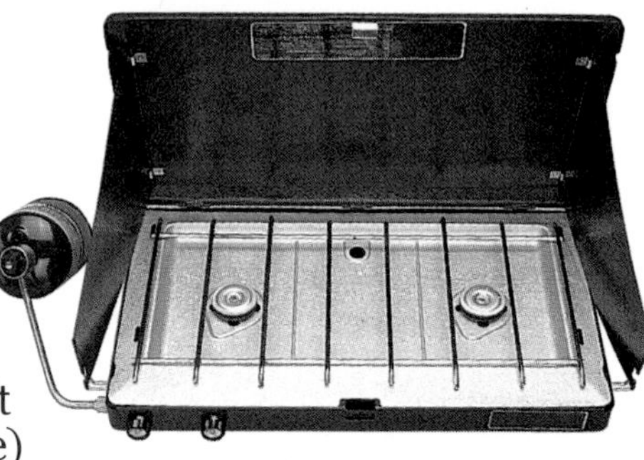

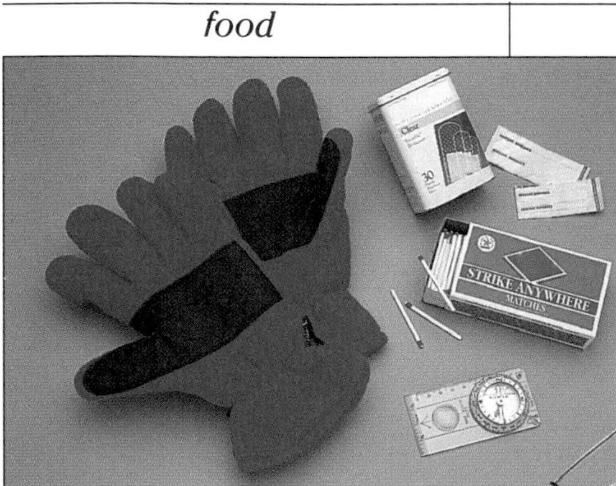

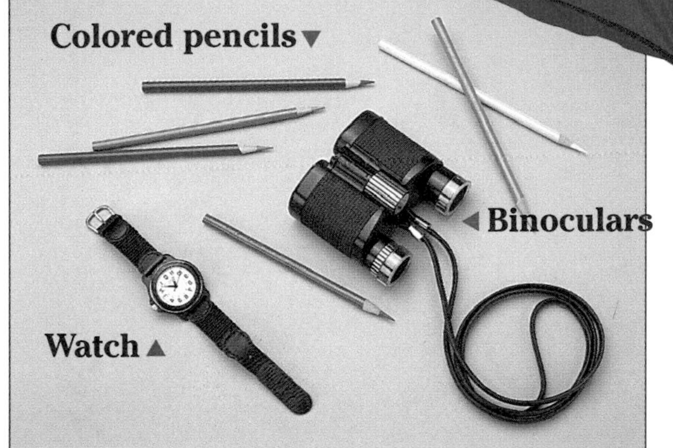

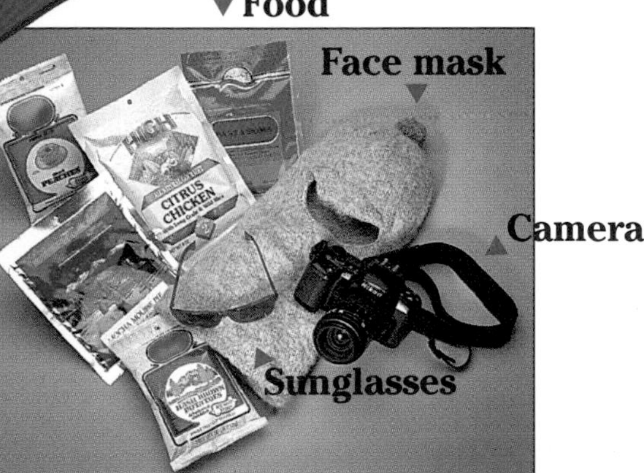

Language Focus

Q: Why did they take tents?
A: To stay warm at night.

b. Share ideas with your classmates.

c. Pairwork. Why did the explorers take these items on their trip? Write your ideas in a chart. Then compare ideas with your classmates.

Why did they take . . . ?	
tents	*To stay warm at night*
binoculars	
sleeping bags	
colored pencils	

9. Compute

a. On your own. Look back at the reading to find answers to these questions:

1. How many days did it take to cross Antarctica?
2. How many miles did the explorers travel each day?

b. How many miles did the explorers travel in all? Use the formula below to find the answer.

Formula: Distance equals rate (number of miles per day) multiplied by the time.

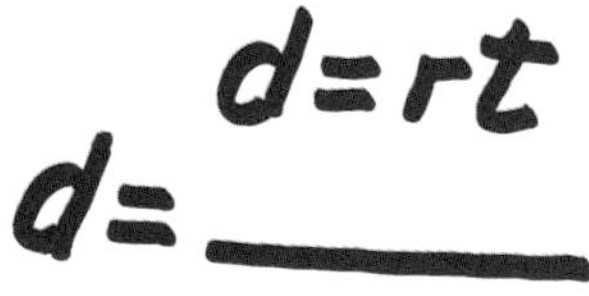

10. Plan

a. Groupwork. Traveling across Antarctica on skis is challenging, or difficult to do. Follow the instructions below to plan another challenging trip.

1. Choose a place for your trip. Draw your route on a map.
2. Describe this area in a chart like this:

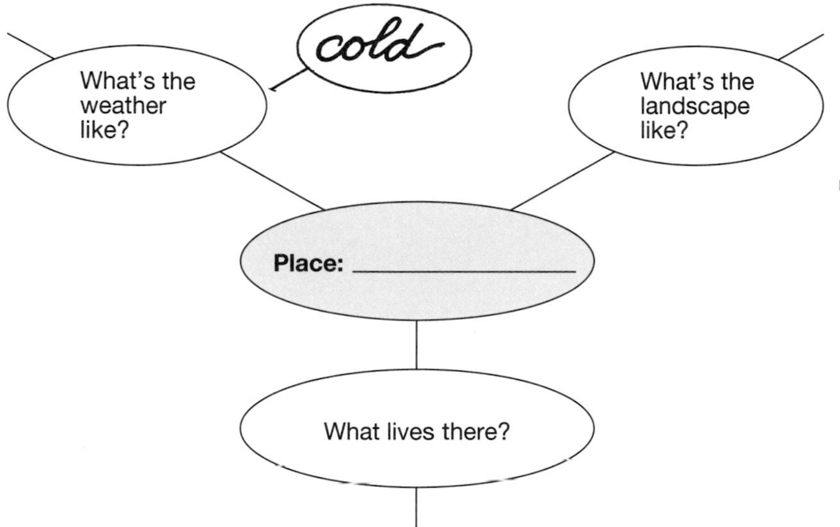

Language Focus

- We will travel by boat.
- We will take a tent.

3. Answer the questions in a chart like this.

How will you travel?	
What will you take with you?	
What will be challenging about your trip?	

b. Share your plan with the class. Each person in your group can tell something about your plan.

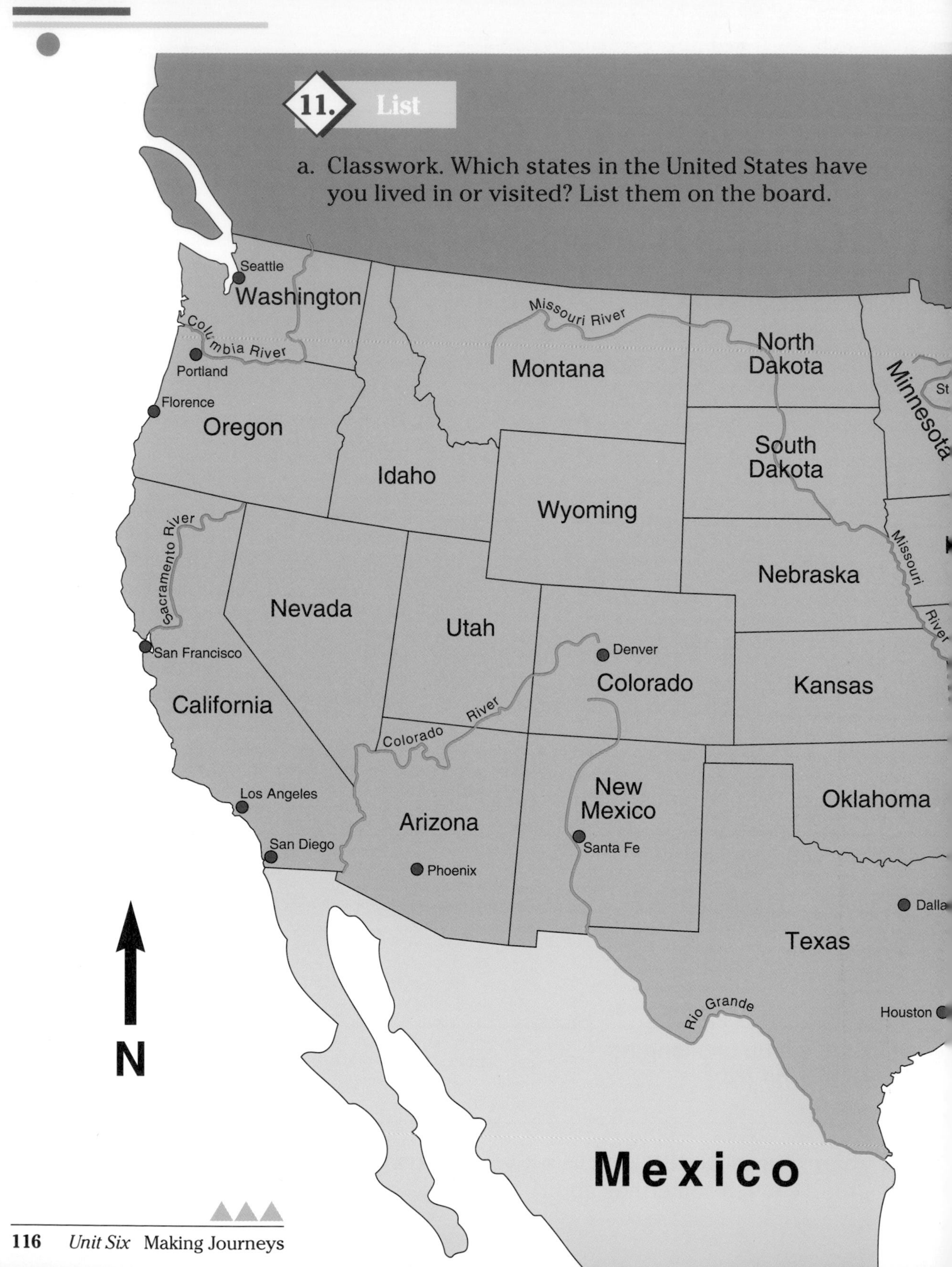

a. Classwork. Which states in the United States have you lived in or visited? List them on the board.

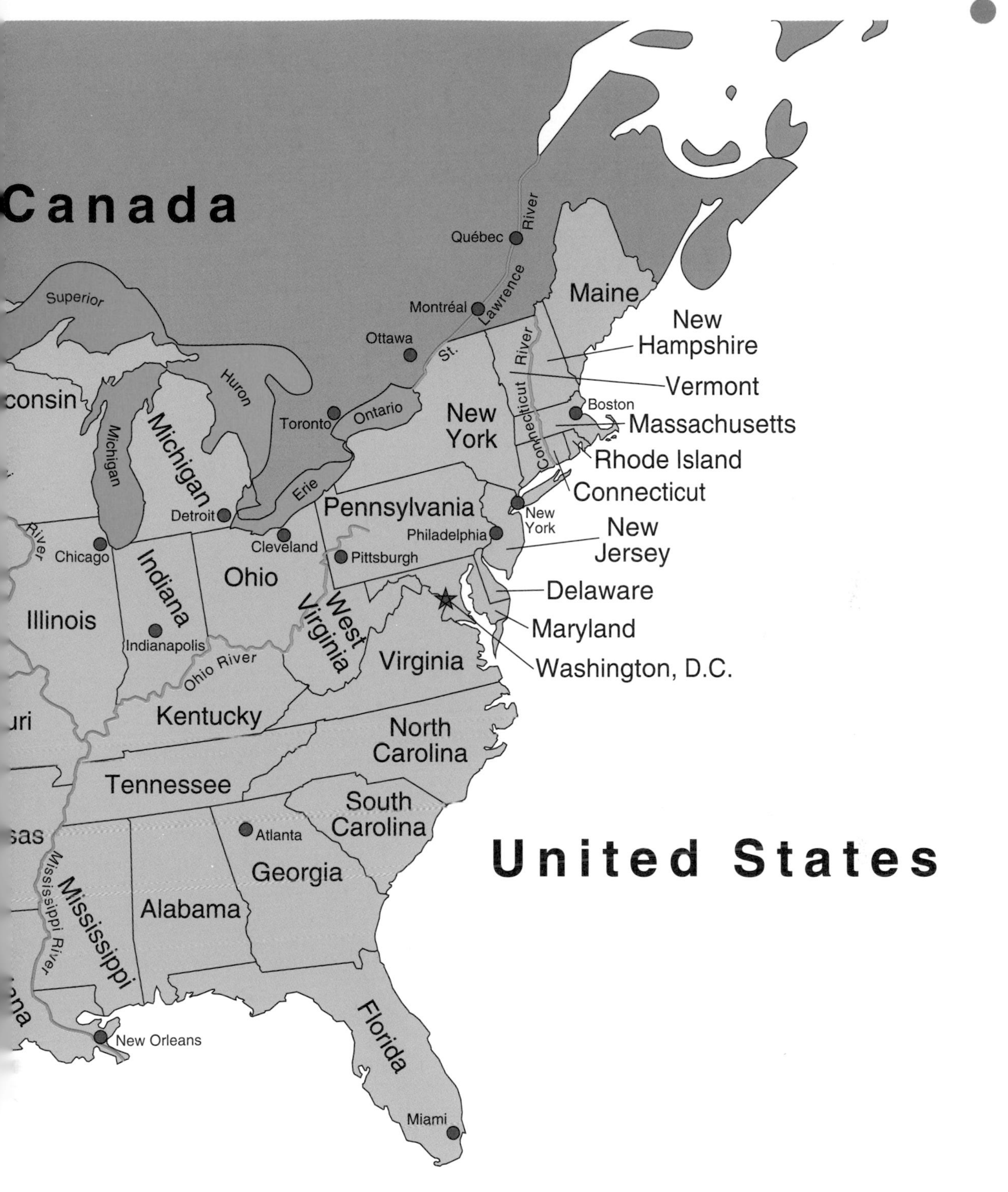
Canada
Québec
St. Lawrence River
Superior
Montréal
Ottawa
Maine
New Hampshire
Vermont
Connecticut River
Boston
Massachusetts
Rhode Island
Connecticut
consin
Huron
Michigan
Michigan
Toronto
Ontario
New York
Erie
Detroit
Pennsylvania
New York
New Jersey
Philadelphia
River
Chicago
Cleveland
Pittsburgh
Indiana
Ohio
West Virginia
Delaware
Illinois
Maryland
Indianapolis
Ohio River
Virginia
Washington, D.C.
Kentucky
uri
North Carolina
Tennessee
South Carolina
sas
Atlanta
United States
Georgia
Mississippi River
Mississippi
Alabama
Florida
na
New Orleans
Miami

b. Classwork. Group the states on your list. Most states will fit into more than one group. Then answer the question below.

The United States

North (northern part)	South (southern part)	East (eastern part)	West (western part)	Center (central part)
Oregon	*Alabama*	*New York*	*California*	*Missouri*
New York	*California*		*Oregon*	

Which part of the United States does your class know best?

Language Focus

- California is in the western part of the United States.
- California is in the southern part of the United States.
- California is in the southwestern part of the United States.

c. Classwork. Study the map on page 119. Which provinces in Canada have you lived in or visited? List them on the board.

d. Classwork. Group the provinces in Canada on your list. Then answer the question below.

Canada

North (northern part)	South (southern part)	East (eastern part)	West (western part)	Center (central part)
	Manitoba	*Quebec*		*Manitoba*

Which part of Canada does your class know best?

Language Focus

Q: Where's Montreal?
A: It's in the eastern part of Canada.
Q: Where's San Diego?
A: It's in the western part of the United States.

Language Focus

Q: Where will you go from Montreal?
A: From Montreal, we'll go to Ottawa, Ontario.

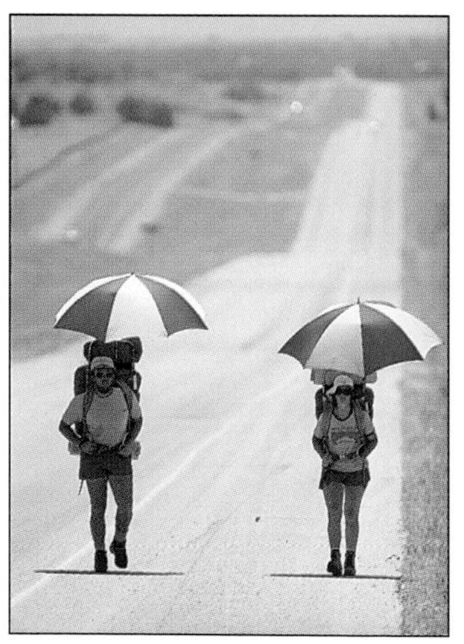

12. Locate

a. Classwork. Take a trip by car from Montreal, Quebec, to San Diego, California. Visit the cities below on your trip. Locate them on the map on pages 116-117.

- Chicago, Illinois
- Kansas City, Missouri
- Montreal, Quebec
- Ottawa, Ontario
- Phoenix, Arizona
- San Diego, California
- Santa Fe, New Mexico
- St. Paul, Minnesota

b. Groupwork. What route will you take from Montreal to San Diego? Draw it on a map. Then answer the questions below.

1. How many provinces in Canada will you travel through?
2. How many states in the United States will you travel through?
3. What large rivers will you cross?

c. Compare routes with another group.

13. Jigsaw

a. Classwork. In 1976, Barbara and Peter Jenkins walked from New Orleans, Louisiana, to Florence, Oregon. Find these places on the map on page 116.

b. Pairwork. Student A looks at page 121 only. Student B looks at page 122 only. Ask your partner for information.

Student A: Ask your partner questions to complete the Jenkins' route from New Orleans to Florence.

Example:

You: Where did they go from *New Orleans* ?

Your partner: From New Orleans, they went to Westlake.

You: Where's *Westlake* ?

Your partner: It's in the western part of Louisiana.

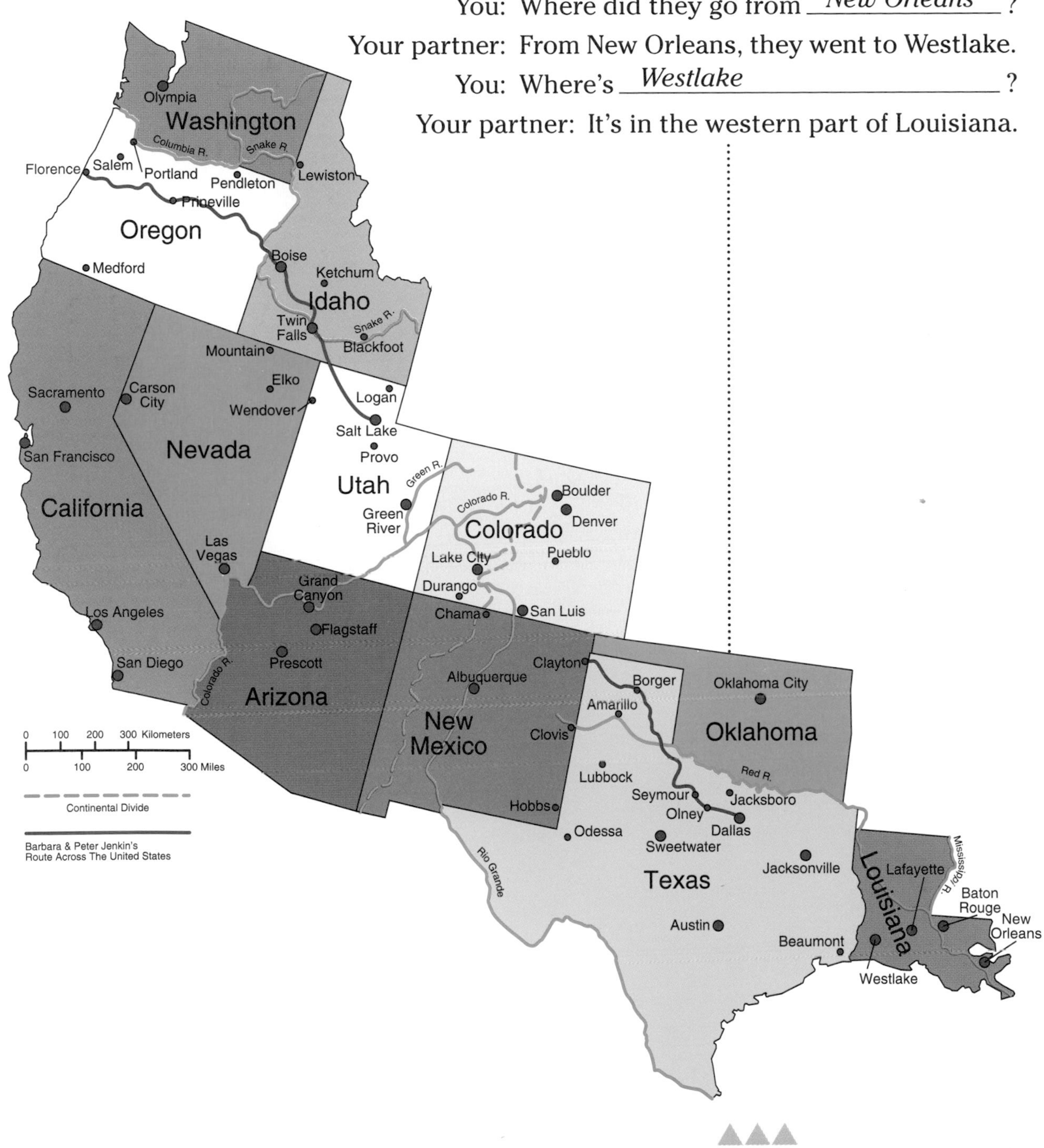

Student B: Ask your partner questions to complete the Jenkins' route from New Orleans to Florence.

Example:

You: Where did they go from *Dallas*?

Your partner: From Dallas they went to Olney.

You: Where's *Olney*?

Your partner: It's in northern Texas.

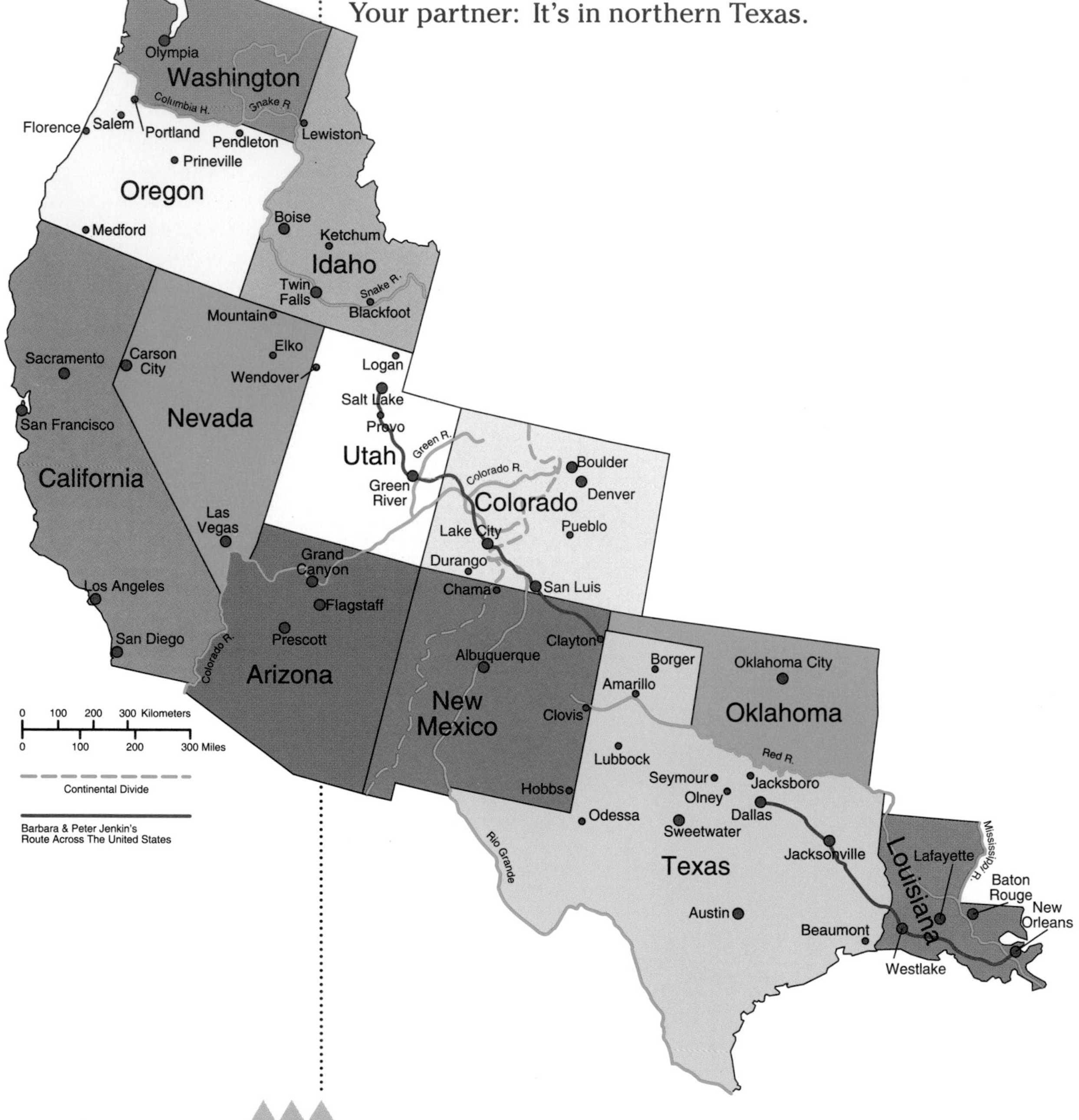

c. Compare maps with your partner. Then answer these questions:

1. How many states did they travel through?
2. Which rivers did they cross?
3. Which mountains did they cross?
4. Find the Continental Divide on the map on page 122. (It's a dotted line.)

Where did Barbara and Peter Jenkins cross the Continental Divide?

 14. Describe

a. Groupwork. Choose one picture. Find the place on the map on page 122.

These pictures show places that Barbara and Peter Jenkins visited on their trip across the United States.

The Cascade Range in Oregon between Salem and Prineville.

The Continental Divide

The Continental Divide is an imaginary line that runs along the Rocky Mountains. Most streams on the western side of this line eventually drain into the Pacific Ocean. Most streams on the eastern side drain into the Atlantic Ocean.

The Book Cliffs in eastern Utah

Oil fields in western Texas

b. Groupwork. Write about the place in your picture.

Example:

Place: ______________

Where is it?	
What's the weather like?	
What's the landscape like?	

c. Show the class where this place is on the map. Tell them about it.

Activity Menu

Choose one of the following activities to do.

1. What's it like there?
Write about a country you have lived in. Here are some questions you might answer in your writing:

- Where is this country?
- What's the weather like?
- What's the landscape like?

Share your writing with your classmates.

2. Plan a trip
Plan a trip from North America to another country far away. Tell how you can get there. Draw the route on a map. Show your route to your classmates.

3. Describe a trip
Tell your classmates about a trip you took. Show your route on a map. Tell about any problems you had. Answer any questions your classmates have.

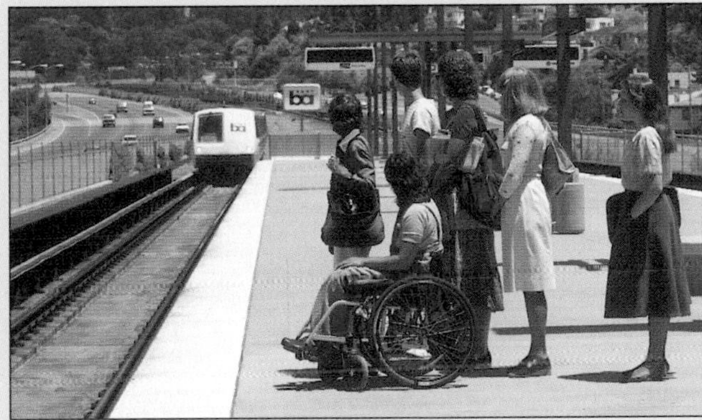

4. Read a magazine article
In a library, find a copy of the November 1990 issue of *National Geographic* magazine. Turn to page 67 and study the pictures of the International Expedition to Antarctica. Look for information about the trip across the continent. Share what you learned with your classmates.

5. Collect information
Choose one of the states in the United States or provinces in Canada. Collect information about this state or province to share with your classmates. Study a map in an atlas. Look up information in an encyclopedia.

Language Focus
Raul couldn't understand his teachers.
Hanh couldn't eat the ________.

Solving Problems

1. Listen

a. Classwork. Listen and complete the sentences.

These students moved to North America last year. What problems did they have when they arrived here?

1. Raul: I couldn't understand my ______.
2. Alicia: I didn't know anyone at ______.
3. Ahmed: People couldn't say my ______.
4. Hanh: I couldn't eat the ______. It was very different from the ______ in my country.
5. Boris: I didn't speak ______ very well.
6. Rosalva: Sometimes I got ______.

b. Report what you learned.

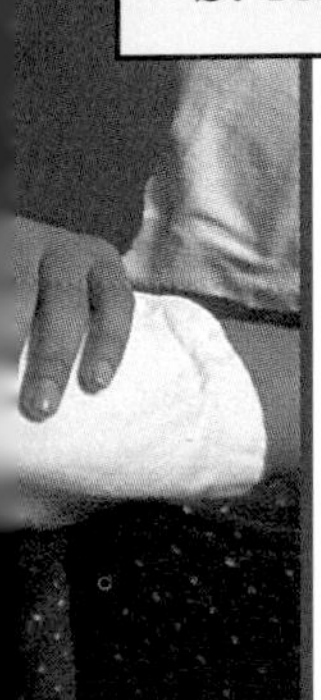

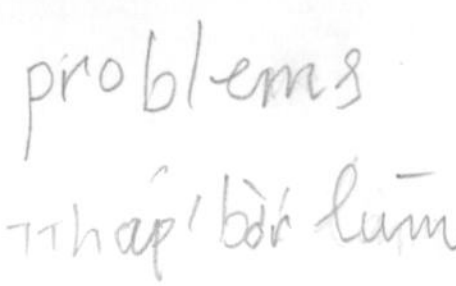

2. Think-Pair-Share

a. On your own. Think about your first days in this country. What problems did you have?

b. Pairwork. Tell your partner about your first days in this country. Listen carefully to your partner's story.

c. Get together with another pair. Tell about your partner's first days in this country.

Language Focus

- I couldn't ________ .
- I didn't ________ .

3. Predict

Classwork. The story below tells about one student's first day at a new school. What problems do you think she had? List your ideas.

What problems did she have on her first day at school?

____

____

____

Language Focus

- Maybe she got lost.
- Maybe she didn't know anyone.

4. Shared Reading

My First Day at School

My first day at this school was January 15, 1992. When I got to school, I went to the office. The counselor in the office gave me a class schedule. I couldn't find my homeroom so she took me there. I was really happy in this class because all of the students spoke Spanish. When homeroom finished, my new friends helped me to find my next class. When I got to this class, there were only two students, and they didn't speak Spanish. I was really nervous because I didn't speak English very well. I tried to relax and do my best, but it wasn't easy.

At noon, I had to go to the cafeteria, but I didn't know where it was. I didn't see any Spanish-speaking

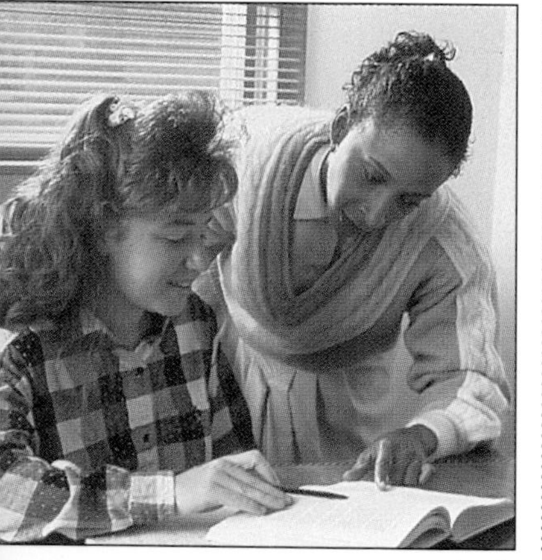

students in the hallway, so I asked a teacher. He told me that the cafeteria was on the first floor. After lunch, I had three more classes. Many students spoke Russian, and I couldn't understand them. I tried to speak English with them, and they seemed friendly. After school, I went home. This was my first day in school.

—*Elena*

5. List

a. On your own. Where did Elena go on her first day at school? List ideas from the reading.

First, she *went to the office* ____________.

Then, she went ____________.

Next, ____________.

After that, ____________.

After lunch, ____________.

After school, ____________.

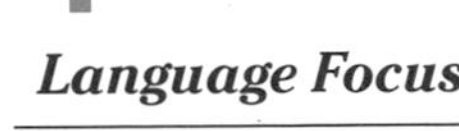

Language Focus

- First, she went to the office.
- Then, she went ____________.

b. Pairwork. Compare lists with your partner.

6. Answer Questions

a. Pairwork. Answer the questions in a chart like this.

What problems did Elena have?	What did she do?
She couldn't find her homeroom.	*The counselor took her there.*
She couldn't find her next class.	
She was nervous because she didn't speak English well.	
She couldn't find the cafeteria.	

b. Pairwork. Compare answers with your partner.

7. Write

a. On your own. What problems did you have on your first day at this school? List your ideas in a chart like this.

What problems did you have?	What did you do?

b. On your own. Use the ideas in your chart to write about your first day at this school.

c. Pairwork. Read your story to your partner. Listen carefully to your partner's story. Take notes in a chart like this.

What problems did your partner have?	What did your partner do?

d. Get together with another pair. Tell them about your partner's first day at school.

8. Predict

Classwork. In the story on pages 132–134, a man wants to build an oven, but he has a problem. What do you think is the problem? Make a prediction.

Maybe ______________________

____

____

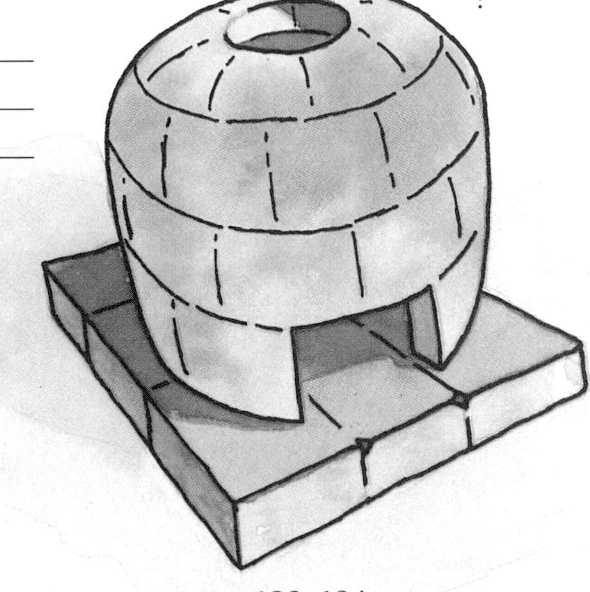

9. Analyze

a. Groupwork. Choose a picture on pages 132–134. Write several questions about the picture.

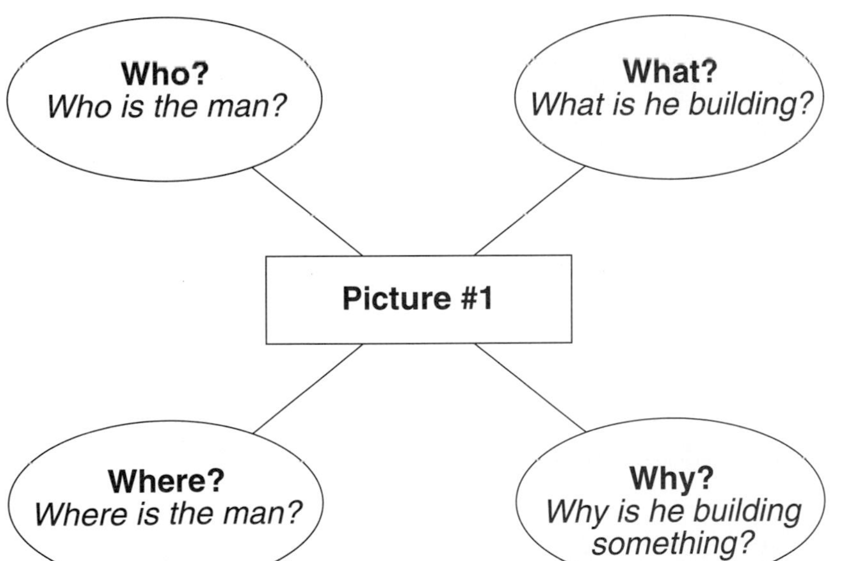
Who?
Who is the man?
What?
What is he building?
Picture #1
Where?
Where is the man?
Why?
Why is he building something?

b. Read your questions to the class. Let them guess answers to your questions.

Nasr-ed-Din's Oven

NARRATOR: Fatima and her husband, Nasr-ed-Din, lived in a small village. They didn't have an oven at home, so several times a week, Fatima baked her bread in the village oven.

FATIMA: I'm tired of going to the village oven to bake my bread. Some of my friends have ovens at home. Setare has a fine clay oven. Turan has an oven, too. And so does Ina.

NASR-ED-DIN: If you want an oven at home, I'll build one. I'll build it tomorrow.

NARRATOR: The next day, Nasr-ed-Din built an oven for Fatima. In the evening, his neighbor Ali came over to visit. Ali walked all around the new oven, shaking his head.

NASR-ED-DIN: What's wrong?

ALI: Your oven faces east.

NASR-ED-DIN: So what?

ALI: Don't you know which way the wind blows? An oven facing east is no good. The wind will put out your fire.

1

2

NARRATOR: The next morning, Nasr-ed-Din tore apart the oven. Then he built it again, facing west. He worked hard all day, and by evening, the oven was finished. He was admiring his new oven when his friend Daoud came over. Daoud walked all around the oven, shaking his head.

3

4

NASR-ED-DIN: What's wrong?

DAOUD: Your oven faces west.

NASR-ED-DIN: So what?

DAOUD: Don't you know which way the wind usually blows? An oven facing west is no good. There isn't enough air to start a fire.

5

NARRATOR: The next morning, Nasr-ed-Din tore apart his oven again. This time, he built the oven on an old cart with two wheels. He worked hard, and by evening, the oven was finished. Just then, Ali and Daoud came over to visit. They looked at the oven. They walked around it several times.

6

ALI: Why, oh why . . . ?

DAOUD: Why did you build your oven on top of a cart?

NASR-ED-DIN: I built it on a cart so that I can turn it in any direction—north, south, east, or west—whichever way my neighbors want it to face.

11. Share Ideas

Classwork. Share ideas about the story. Here are some questions you might think about.

1. Did you like the story? Why or why not?
2. How many times did Nasr-ed-Din build the oven?
3. How do you think Nasr-ed-Din felt at different times in the story? Why?
4. Do you think Nasr-ed-Din was a good problem solver? Why or why not?

12. Role Play

Groupwork. Get together in groups of five. Act out the story "Nasr-ed-Din's Oven."

13. Make a Plot Profile

a. Pairwork. What happened in the story? Add to the list of events below.

List of Events

1. Fatima asked Nasr-ed-Din to build an oven.
2. Nasr-ed-Din built an oven.
3. Ali came over.
4. Ali said the oven shouldn't face east.
5. Nasr-ed-Din tore apart the oven.
6. ______________________________
7. ______________________________
8. ______________________________
9. ______________________________
10. ______________________________
11. ______________________________
12. ______________________________

b. Pairwork. Think about the first event in the story. How interesting is it? Choose a number from 1 (not interesting) to 10 (very interesting). Put a dot next to this number in the first column of a plot profile chart like this.

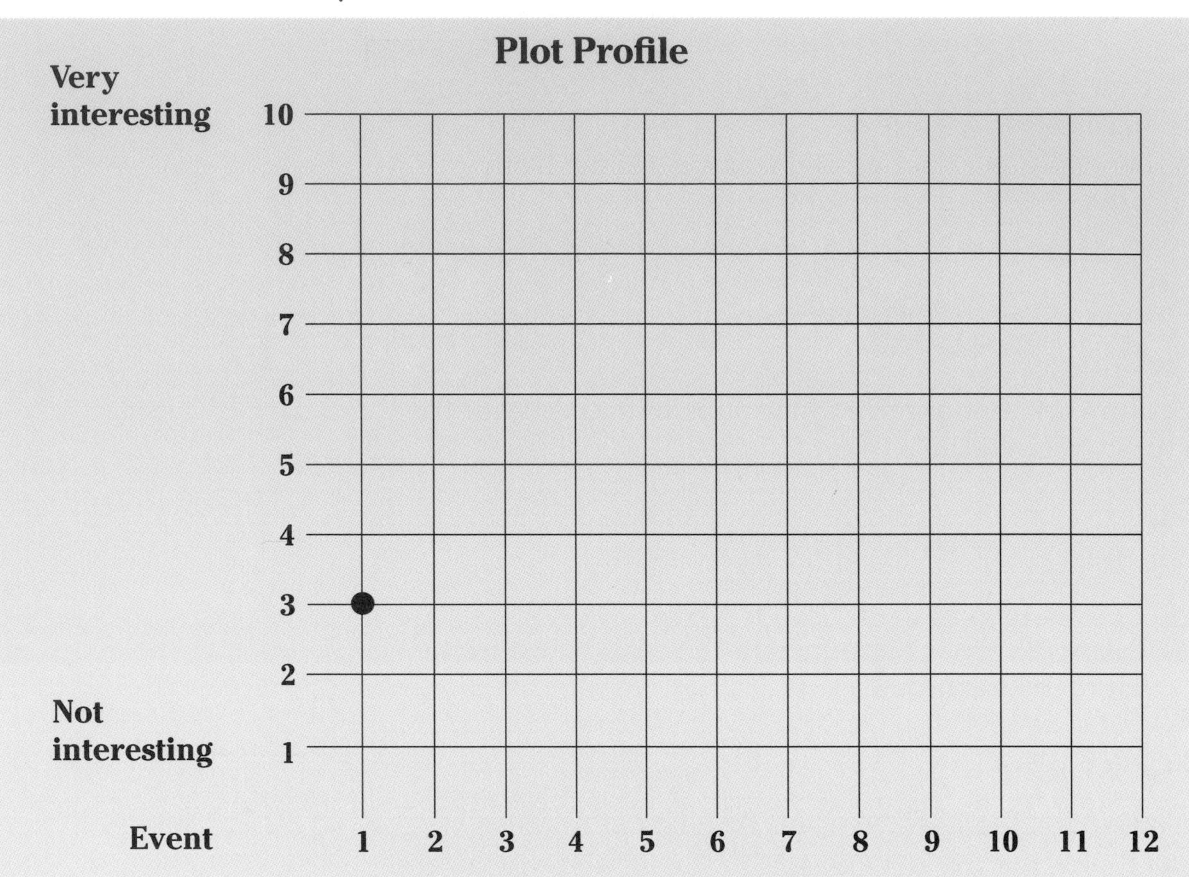

c. Repeat with the remaining events in the story. Then connect the dots.

d. Compare plot profiles with another pair.

14. Identify

a. Pairwork. What problems did Nasr-ed-Din have? How did he solve the problems? List your ideas in a chart like this.

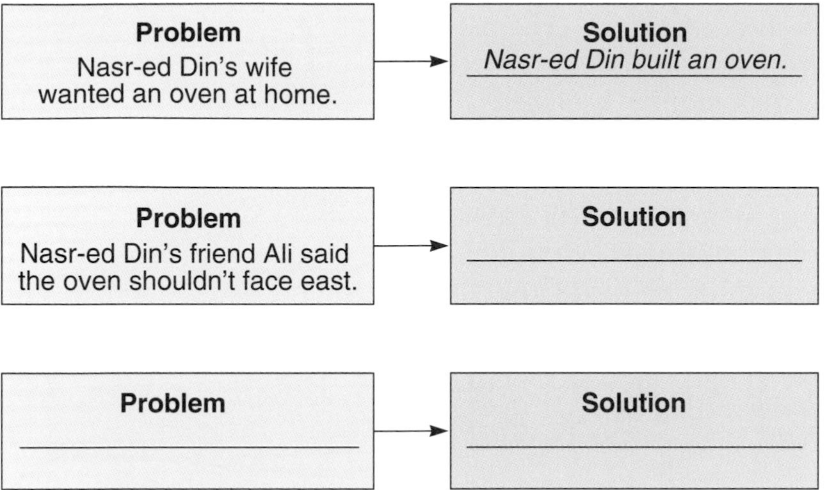

Problem		Solution
Nasr-ed Din's wife wanted an oven at home.	→	*Nasr-ed Din built an oven.*
Nasr-ed Din's friend Ali said the oven shouldn't face east.	→	______________
______________	→	______________

b. Compare charts with another pair.

15. Guess

Classwork. Study the pictures on pages 138–140. In each picture, someone has a problem. What do you think the problem is?

Picture #1: ______________________________

____

Picture #2: ______________________________

____

Picture #3: ______________________________

____

Language Focus

- Maybe the people don't like the man's ice cream.
- Maybe the man doesn't like to work outdoors.

Shared Reading

> ***Language Focus***
>
> - Maybe he bought more bowls.
> - Maybe he put the ice cream in cups.

a. Groupwork. Read about these three problems. For each problem, think of several possible solutions.

Problem 1	**Possible Solutions**
In 1904, Charles Menches sold bowls of ice cream from his outdoor ice cream stand. One very hot day, many people wanted to buy ice cream, but Menches didn't have enough bowls. What do you think he did? How did he solve his problem?	______________________ ______________________ ______________________

Problem 2

A hundred years ago, many people wore shoes with buttons. It took a long time to fasten these shoes because they had a lot of buttons. Whitcomb Judson had a friend with a bad back. His friend couldn't button his shoes because his back hurt. Judson wanted to help his friend. What do you think he did?

Possible Solutions

____

____

____

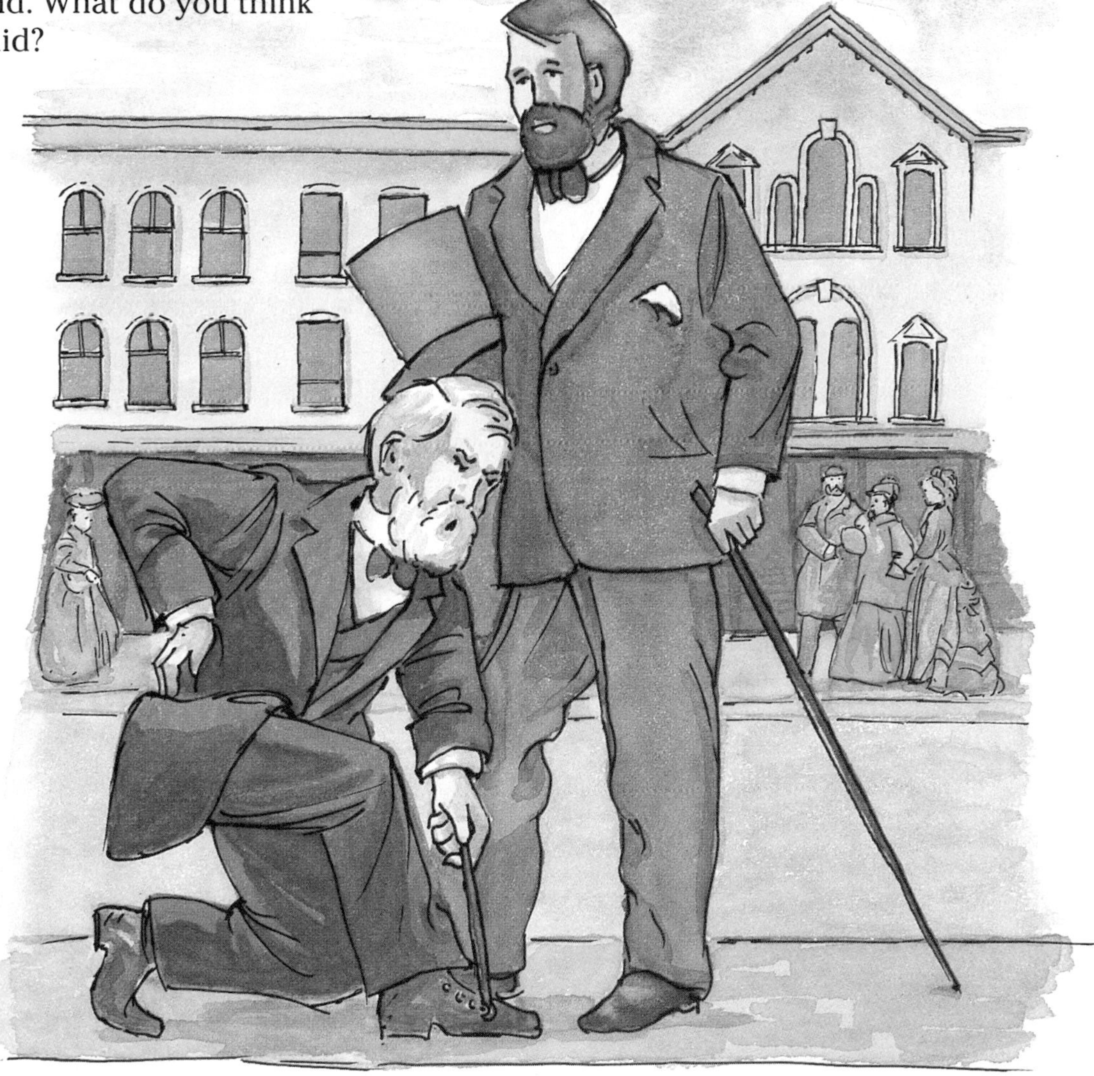

Problem 3

In 1848, a salesman traveled from New York to California. He took with him a large supply of canvas. Canvas is a very heavy material that people use to make tents. Thc salesman hoped to sell the canvas to gold prospectors—people who dig for gold. When he arrived in California, however, the prospectors didn't need tents. No one wanted to buy his canvas. What do you think he did?

Possible Solutions

___

___

___

b. Read your lists of possible solutions to the class.

c. Compare your ideas with these solutions.

1. Next to Menches' ice cream stand, a man by the name of Ernest Hamwi was selling zalabia—a thin Persian waffle. Hamri rolled one of his waffles into a cone shape, and Menches put a scoop of ice cream into it. It was the first ice cream cone.

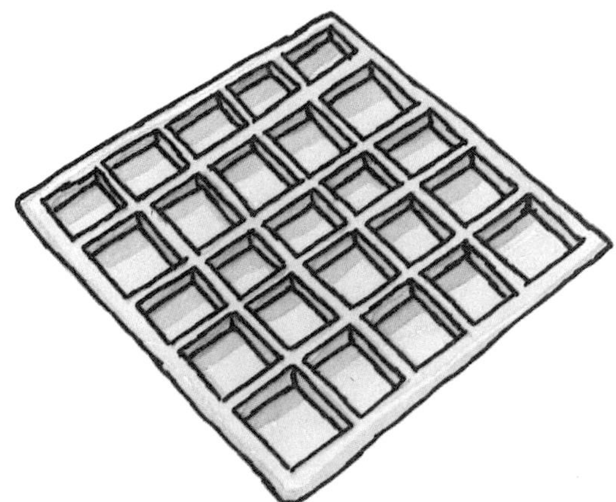

2. Whitcomb Judson came up with the idea for the zipper. With one hand, his friend could quickly fasten his shoes.

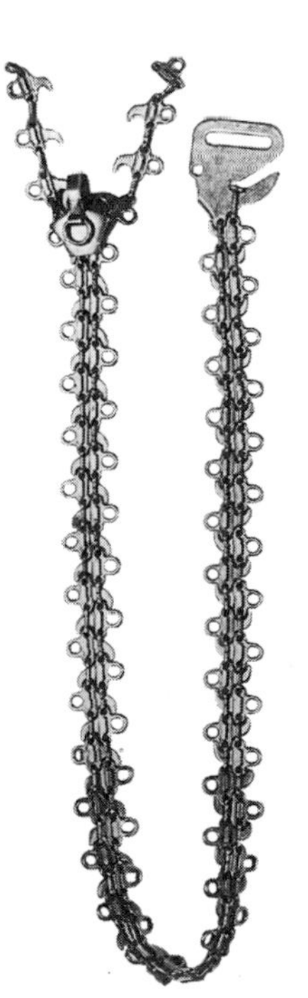

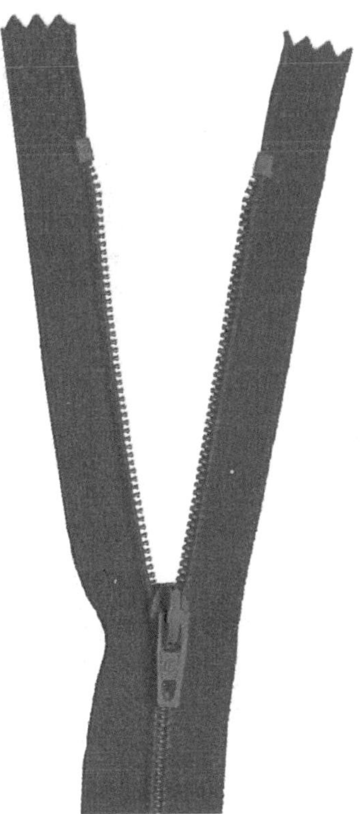

3. The salesman noticed that the prospectors frequently bought new pants. Digging for gold was hard work, and the prospectors' pants wore out quickly. The salesman decided to use his canvas to make pants. The prospectors liked his canvas pants because they were very strong. The salesman's name was Levi Strauss, and these pants were the first jeans.

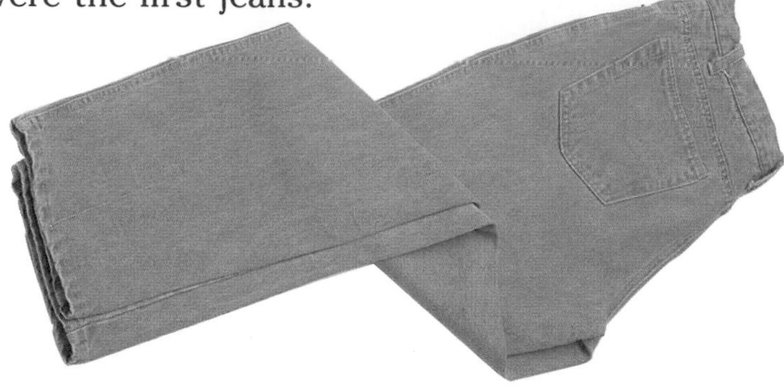

17. Make a Chart

a. Groupwork. Use the information on pages 138–142 to complete a chart like this.

Name	What problem did he have?	How did he solve the problem?
Charles Menches	*He didn't have the bowls to put his ice cream in.*	
Whitcomb Judson		
Levi Strauss		

b. Get together with another group. Take turns asking questions.

Q: What problem did ______________________ have?
A: ______________________________.
Q: How did he solve this problem?
A: ______________________________.

18. Design

a. Classwork. Read the information below.

During World War I (1914–1918), soldiers wore helmets like this:

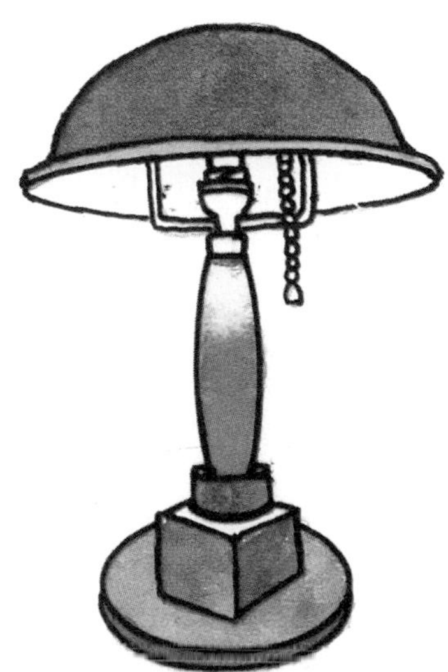

After the war, the soldiers didn't need these helmets. To find new uses for the helmets, the magazine *Popular Mechanics* had a contest. It asked people to think of new ways to use the helmets. Here's one example:

b. Groupwork. What are some other ways to use these helmets? List your ideas.

You could use the helmets ______________________________

____.

c. Groupwork. Choose one of your ideas. Draw a picture to illustrate it. Share your drawing with the class.

19. Guess

Classwork. What is the contraption or strange looking machine on the next page? What could you do with it? Share ideas with your classmates.

20. Shared Reading

a. Classwork. Listen to this poem. Then read it aloud with your classmates.

Homework Machine

The Homework Machine, oh, the Homework Machine,
Most perfect contraption that's ever been seen.
Just put in your homework, then drop in a dime,
Snap on the switch, and in ten seconds' time,
Your homework comes out, quick and clean as can be.
Here it is—"nine plus four?" and the answer is "three."
Three?
Oh me . . .
I guess it's not as perfect
As I thought it would be.

—*Shel Silverstein*

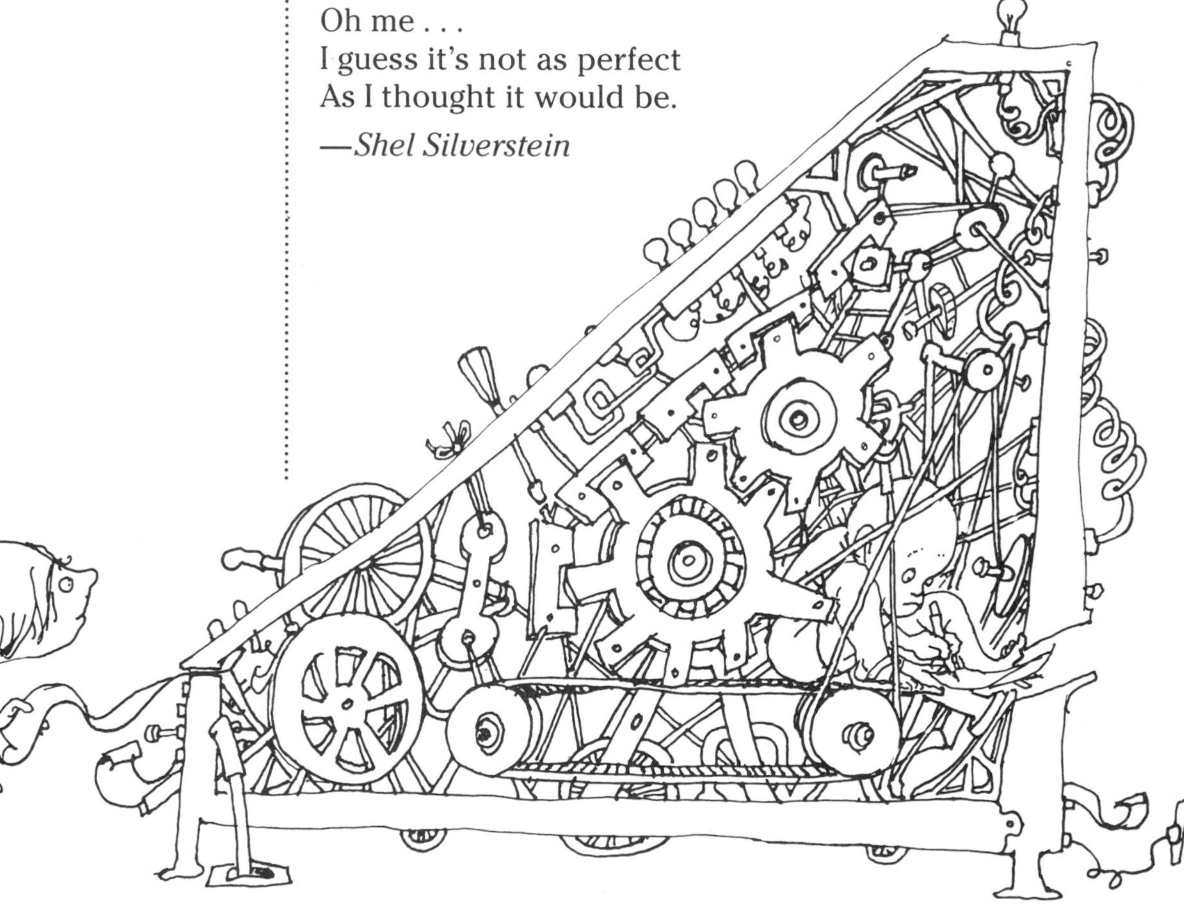

b. Classwork. Act out the poem.

21. Analyze

Pairwork. How does the homework machine work? List the steps.

1. First, *put in your homework* ____________.
2. Then, ________________________.
3. Next, ________________________.
4. In the end, *your homework comes out* ____________.

Language Focus

- Put in ________.
- Snap on ________.
- Turn on ________.
- Drop in ________.

22. Write

a. Groupwork. What kind of contraption would you like to have? Name it below.

The ____________________ Machine

b. Groupwork. What problem does your machine solve? Write a sentence telling what it does.

____

____

c. Groupwork. How does your contraption work? List the steps.

1. First, ________________________.
2. Then, ________________________.
3. Next, ________________________.
4. Then, ________________________.
5. In the end, ________________________.

d. Groupwork. Use your ideas to write a poem. Then read your poem to the class.

Activity Menu

Choose one of the following activities to do.

1. How Does It Work? 

Bring to class a tool, kitchen gadget, or other piece of equipment. Teach your classmates how to use it. Together, think of other things you could use it for.

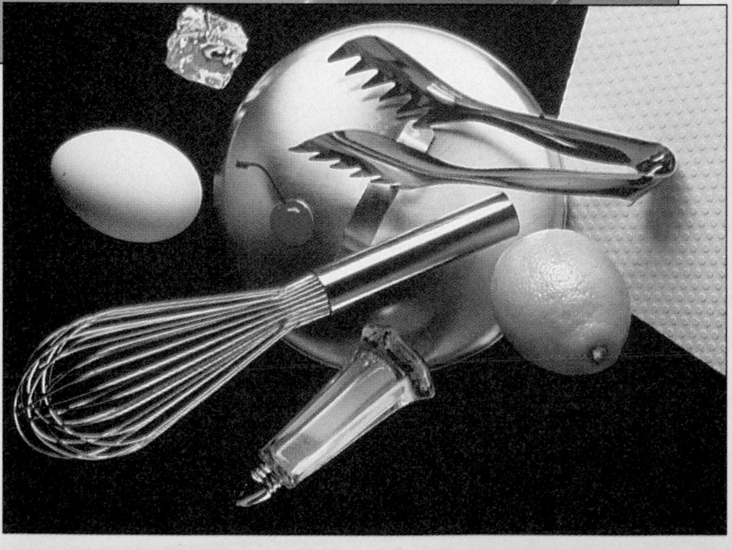

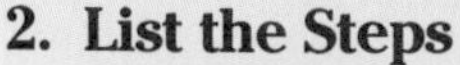

2. List the Steps

Watch someone use one of these machines:

- a copy machine
- a pay phone
- a fax machine
- a video recorder

List the steps for using the machine. Then act out the steps for your classmates.

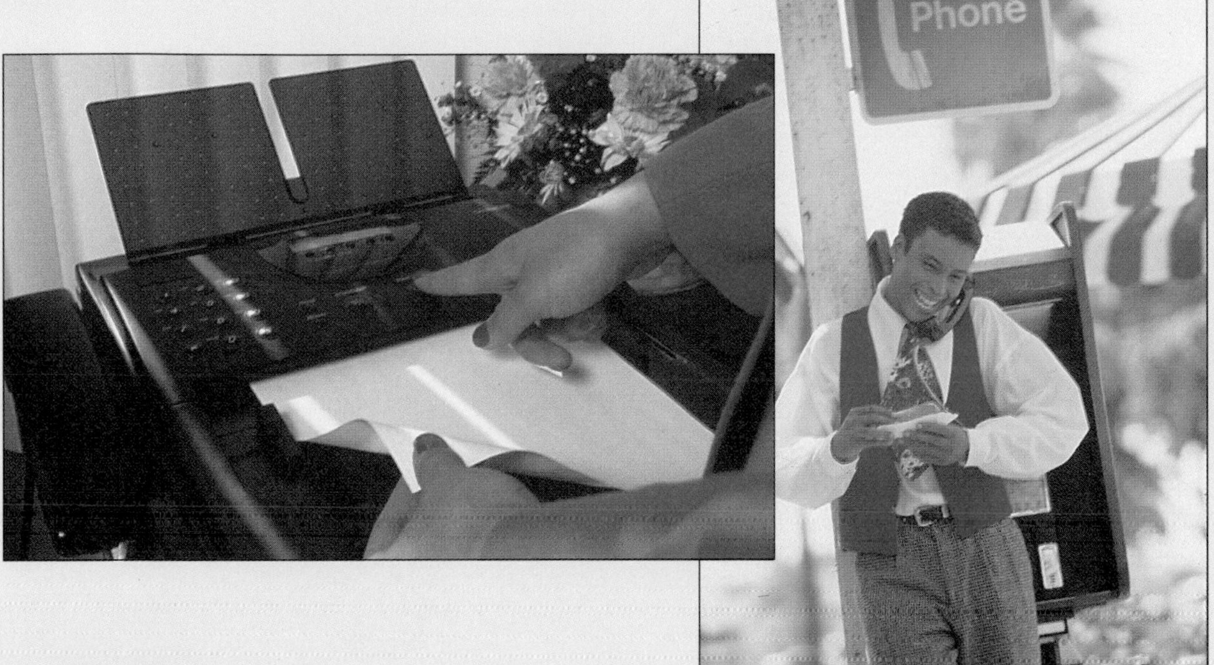

3. Tell a Story

Write or retell a story. Read it to your classmates. Then ask them to make a plot profile of the story.

4. What's Your Advice?

List some of the problems newcomers to the United States might have. For each problem, tell what you could do to solve the problem. Put your ideas together in a booklet for newcomers. Give a copy of the booklet to your school counselor.

5. Find Out about an Invention

Look up the word *inventions* in the card catalog in a library. How many books about inventions are there? Choose one of the books and read about one invention. Tell the class what problem this invention solves. What does it help you to do?

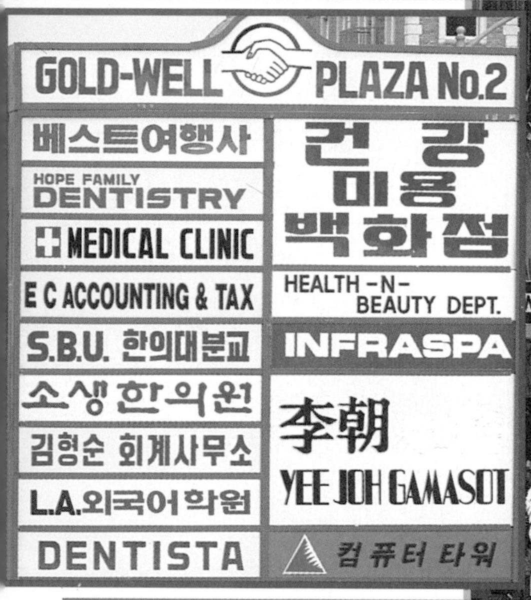

GOLD-WELL PLAZA No.2
베스트여행사
HOPE FAMILY DENTISTRY
MEDICAL CLINIC
E C ACCOUNTING & TAX
S.B.U. 한의대분교
소생한의원
김형순 회계사무소
L.A.외국어학원
DENTISTA
건강 미용 백화점
HEALTH -N- BEAUTY DEPT.
INFRASPA
李朝
YEE JOH GAMASOT
컴퓨터 타워

College Republicans for
President
BUSH
We the People...
TAKE BACK AMERICA
BROWN FOR PRESIDENT
THE REAL
EDUCATION
Bill Clinton
BUSH
92

5995

Exploring Diversity

List

Classwork. *Diversity* means "variety." How many examples of diversity can you find in these pictures? List your ideas.

Examples of diversity:

- *many different languages*
- *many different kinds of clothing*
- ______________________________

2. Interview

Classwork. How are you and you classmates alike? How are you diverse, or different? Follow the instructions below to collect ideas.

a. On your own. Answer the questions in a chart like this.

	My Answers	My Partner's Answers
What languages do you speak?	*English, Spanish*	
Where were you born?	*San Juan, Puerto Rico*	
What is your favorite school subject?		
What is your favorite free time activity?		
Why are you studying English?		

b. Pairwork. Interview your partner. Add your partner's answers to the chart.

c. Pairwork. Which of your answers are the same? Which of your answers are different? Group your answers on a Venn Diagram.

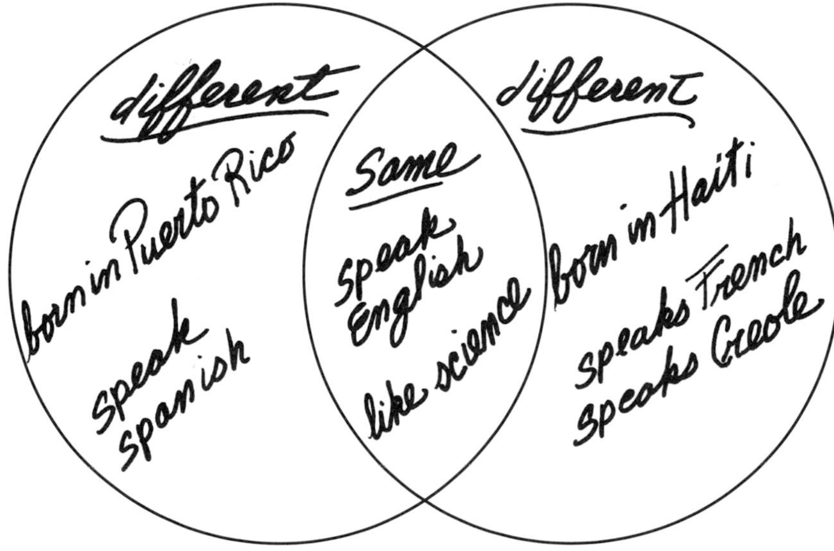

d. Pairwork. Share the information on your Venn Diagram with your classmates.

e. Classwork. Make a class chart on the board. Add information about each person in your class.

Language Focus

Similarities

- We both speak English.
- We both like science best.

Differences

- I speak Spanish and my partner speaks French and Creole.
- I was born in Puerto Rico, but my partner was born in Haiti.

Language	Birthplace	Favorite School Subject	Favorite Free Time Activity	Reasons for Studying English
English French	*Puerto Rico*			

f. Classwork. Count the number of different answers in each category.

g. Classwork. In which category is there the most diversity? In which category is there the least diversity?

Pairwork. Read this information about language diversity in the United States and answer the questions on page 153.

Language Diversity in the United States

Today there are about 230,000,000 people in the United States over the age of five. About fourteen percent of these people speak a language other than English at home. What languages do these people speak? Look at the chart below to find out.

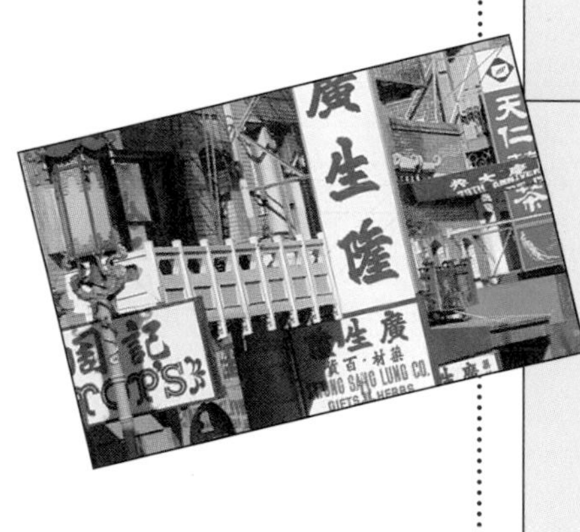

Language Used at Home	Total Speakers Over Five Years Old
Spanish	17,339,000
French	1,703,000
German	1,547,000
Italian	1,309,000
Chinese	1,249,000
Tagalog	843,000
Polish	723,000
Korean	626,000
Vietnamese	507,000
Portuguese	430,000
Japanese	428,000
Greek	388,000
Arabic	355,000
Hindu, Urdu, and related	331,000
Russian	242,000
Yiddish	213,000
Thai	206,000
Persian	202,000
French Creole	188,000
Armenian	150,000
Navaho	149,000
Hungarian	148,000
Hebrew	144,000
Dutch	143,000
Mon-Khmer	127,000

Questions

a. Fourteen percent of the people in the United States over the age of five speak a language other than English at home. How many people is that?

b. On a piece of paper, write your answer to the question in part "a."

   Seventy-five percent of these people say they speak English "well" or "very well." How many people is that?

c. Is your first language listed in the chart? How many people in the United States speak your language?

d. Compare answers with your classmates.

To answer the question in part "a," follow these steps:

1. Reread the paragraph on page 152. Find the number of people in the United States over the age of five.
2. Multiply this number by fourteen percent (.14).

Preview

Classwork. Read the title of the story on the next page and study the pictures. What do you think the characters in the story are saying? Share ideas with your classmates.

5. Shared Reading

Los Ratoncitos

(The Little Mice)

Once upon a time, a mother mouse and her young children went for a walk in the garden. They were looking around for something to eat when they suddenly heard a loud noise. "Hiss, Hiss, Meow!" It was *el gato,* the cat.

The mother mouse told her children to run and hide. The cat ran toward the mother mouse, but she didn't move. Instead, she stood up tall and looked him in the eye. She shook her fist at him. Then she yelled, "Woof, Woof, Woof!"

The cat heard the barking of a dog and was frightened. As quick as a wink, he ran away. The mother mouse called to her children and said, “You see, it’s very important to know a second language.”

6. Share Ideas

Classwork. What is your reaction to the story? Discuss your ideas with your classmates. Here are some questions to think about.

a. Did you like the story? Why or why not?
b. Look again at the pictures. What do you think the mouse is saying? Write your ideas.
c. A bilingual person can speak two languages. What are the advantages of being bilingual?
d. Being bilingual is helpful in many jobs. Can you think of some examples?

7. Make a Story Map

a. On your own. Answer the questions in a story map like this.

Title: ***Los Ratoncitos (The Little Mice)***

Main Characters	**Setting (Place)**
Who is the story about? ______ ______	Where are they? ______ ______

Problem

What is the problem in the story? ______ ______

Plot (Action)

What happened in the beginning of the story?	What happened in the middle of the story?	What happened at the end?
______ ______	______ ______	______ ______ ______

b. Compare story maps with your classmates.

c. Pairwork. Use your story map to retell the story *Los Ratoncitos.* Take turns adding a line to the story.

8.
Write

a. Groupwork. Make up your own story about the importance of learning a second language. Choose animals or people as the characters in your story. Write your ideas in a story map.

Title: ______________________________

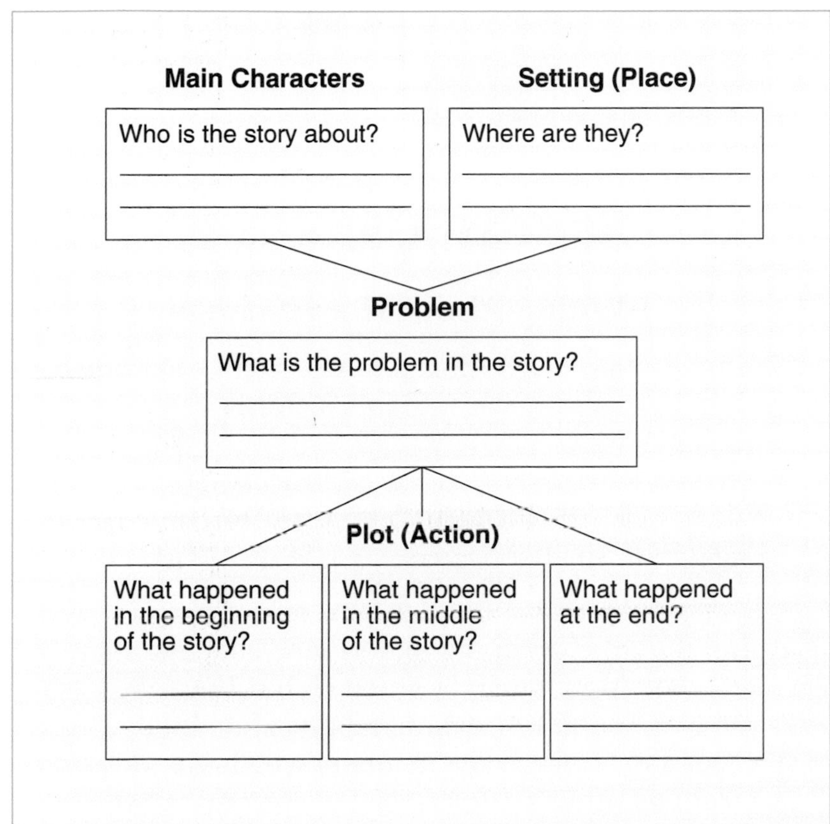
Main Characters
Who is the story about?
Setting (Place)
Where are they?
Problem
What is the problem in the story?
Plot (Action)
What happened in the beginning of the story?
What happened in the middle of the story?
What happened at the end?

b. Write or act out your story for your classmates.

9. Share Ideas

a. Groupwork. Discuss these questions with your classmates.

- What do you think the word *bicultural* means?
- Many people are bilingual. Do you think it is also possible to be bicultural? Why or why not?

b. Report your group's ideas to the class.

10. Use Context

Sandra Cisneros

Writing About Her Heritage

Sandra Cisneros is a Mexican-American poet and writer. In this interview, Cisneros talks about her life and her work.

INTERVIEWER: You grew up bilingual. Do you write in English or Spanish?

CISNEROS: I write in English. But everything I write about comes from my experience as a Spanish-speaker. My English is much richer because I grew up in a Spanish-speaking family. I feel lucky because I have twice as many words to choose from as other writers.

INTERVIEWER: What are your feelings about your Mexican-American heritage?

CISNEROS: My father is from Mexico City, so we visited Mexico a lot when I was growing up. It has always felt like a second home to me. In some ways, I feel more Mexican than American! I get very emotional when I cross the Mexican border or hear the Mexican national anthem.

INTERVIEWER: What would you like your readers to learn from your books?

CISNEROS: People's cultures are what make them special. People should never let go of their roots. My Mexican-American heritage is what made me the writer that I am today. I feel rich because I have two cultures inside of me.

11. Use Context

a. Classwork. Choose a word to complete these sentences. More than one word may be possible.

1. My English is much richer because I grew up in a Spanish-speaking family. I feel ________ because I have twice as many words to choose from as other writers.

   sad happy cold tired smart

   Find the word *lucky* on page 158. What do you think this word means?

2. Mexico has always felt like a second home to me. In some ways I feel more Mexican than American! I get very ________ when I cross the Mexican border, or hear the Mexican national anthem.

   hungry happy sad excited

   Find the word *emotional* on page 158. What do you think this word means?

3. People's cultures are what make them special. People should never let go of their ________. My Mexican-American heritage is what made me the writer that I am today.

   problems culture heritage money family

   Find the word *roots* at the top of this page. What do you think this word means?

12. Take Notes in a Chart

a. Groupwork. What do you know about Sandra Cisneros? Look back at the reading and take notes in a chart like this.

Sandra Cisneros

What is her occupation?	
What languages does she speak?	
How does she feel about being bilingual?	
How does she feel about her heritage (roots)?	
Why does she think roots are important?	

b. Ask your classmates the questions in the chart. Compare answers.

13. Evaluate

a. Groupwork. Do you agree with these ideas? Why or why not?

- People's cultures are what make them special.
- People should never let go of their roots.

b. Report your group's ideas to the class. Tell why you agree or disagree.

14. Study a Picture

a. On your own. This painting gives information about one person's roots. Study the picture for one minute.

Carmen Lomas Garza is a Mexican-American painter. This painting is based on memories of her childhood in Texas.

b. Close your book. List everything you remember about the picture.

Examples: *many people of different ages*
they are outdoors
a dog
two boys are playing marbles

c. Compare lists with your classmates.

d. Pairwork. Look at the picture again. Write several questions about the picture.

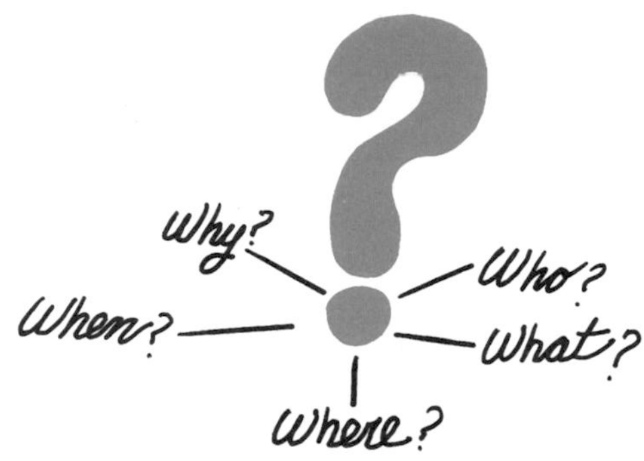

e. Pairwork. Read your questions to the class. (You can point to people in the picture.) Together, think of possible answers.

f. On your own. Carmen Lomas Garza painted a picture of a childhood memory. How would you describe her memory in words? Write your description on another piece of paper.

g. Classwork. What does this painting tell you about Carmen Lomas Garza's roots? What do you know about her? Share ideas with your classmates.

Language Focus

- Who is the girl in the middle?
- What are the two boys in the corner doing?
- Where are these people?
- Why is the girl hitting the fish?

15. Make a Cluster Diagram

a. On your own. What do you remember about your childhood? Follow the steps below to collect your ideas on a cluster diagram.

   1. Think about your childhood. Write anything you think of on a cluster diagram.

My Childhood
Mexico
School

2. Choose one of the ideas on your diagram. What does this idea make you think of? Add these new ideas to the diagram. Think about the ideas in the other circles and write your thoughts about them, too.

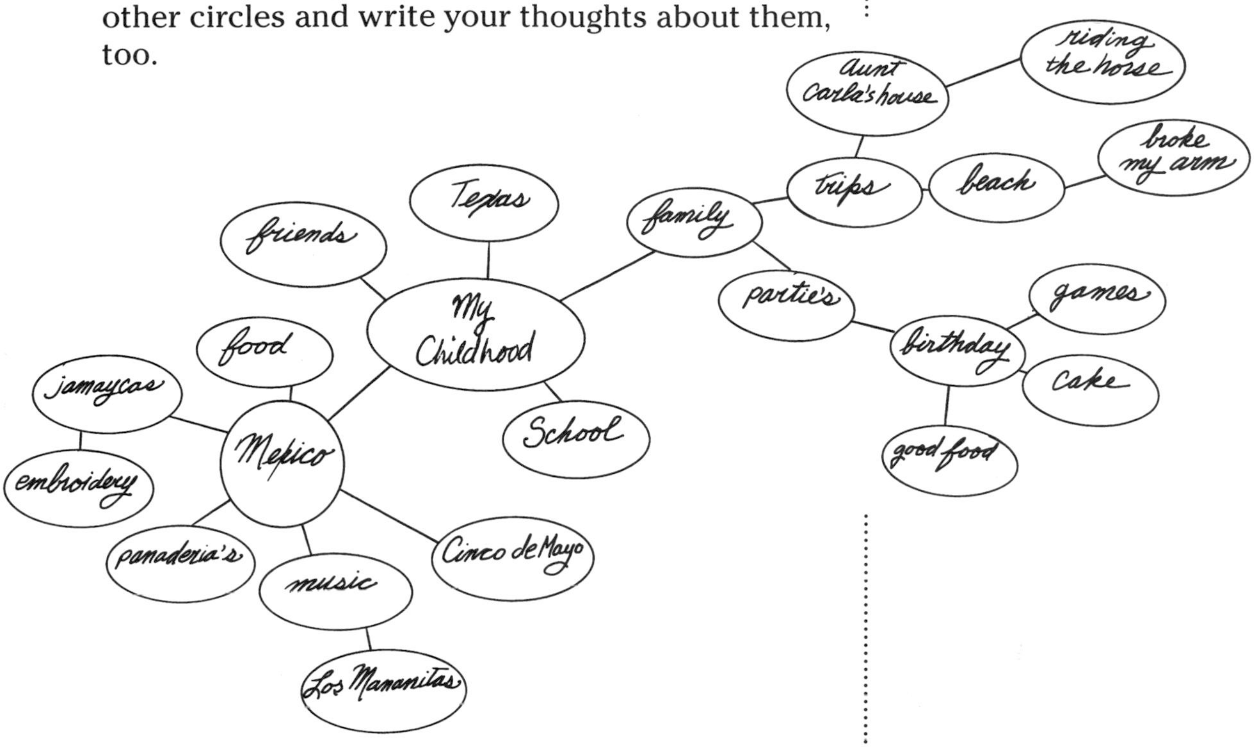

My Childhood
friends
Texas
family
trips
aunt Carla's house
riding the horse
beach
broke my arm
partie's
birthday
games
cake
good food
School
food
Mexico
jamaycas
embroidery
panaderia's
music
Los Mananitas
Cinco de Mayo

16. Think-Pair-Share

a. Pairwork. Choose one of the memories on your cluster diagram. Tell your partner about this special memory. Listen carefully to your partner's story.
b. Ask each other questions about your memories.
c. Get together with another pair. Tell your partner's story.

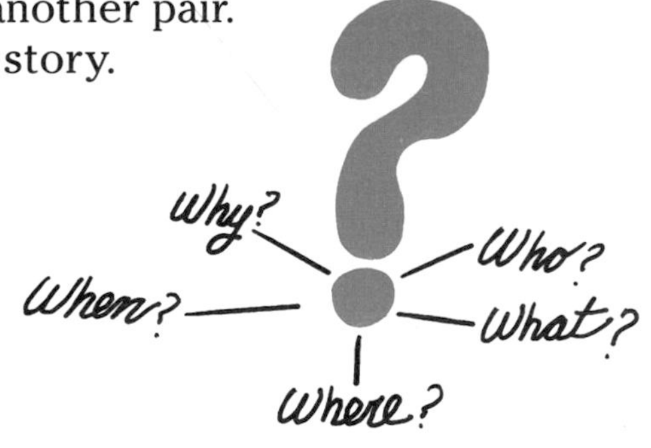

Activity Menu

Choose one of the following activities to do.

1. Make a Collage

Look in magazines for pictures with examples of diversity. Use the pictures to make a collage. Show your collage to your classmates and have them find the examples of diversity.

2. Interview Your Classmates

Interview the people in your class to learn about your similarities and differences. First, prepare a list of questions to ask your classmates. Then collect your classmates' answers. Show the results of your interviews on a chart.

3. Explore Language Diversity at Your School

What languages do the students at your school speak at home? Prepare a questionnaire to collect information. Then give the questionnaire to the students of another class.

4. Interview a Bilingual Person

Interview a bilingual person—someone outside of class. Find out how this person uses two languages. Tell the class what you learned.

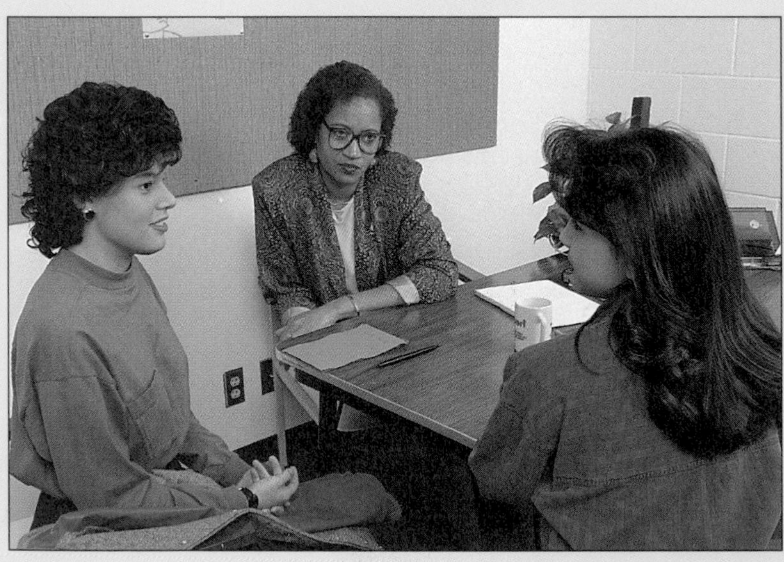

5. Read a Story

Look in a library for the book *The House on Mango Street* by Sandra Cisneros. Read one of the stories in the book and tell your classmates about it.

6. Draw a Picture

Draw a picture of a childhood memory. Show your picture to the class and answer their questions.

7. Collect Words in Different Languages

Choose a word in your first language. Translate this word into any other languages you know. Talk to people who speak other languages. Learn how to say this word in their language. Then find or draw a picture to illustrate this word. Around the picture, list the different ways to say this word.

8. Share Stories

Bring in something from home that gives information about you and your heritage. This might be a photograph, an article of clothing, some food, some music, or a game. Show it to your classmates and answer their questions.

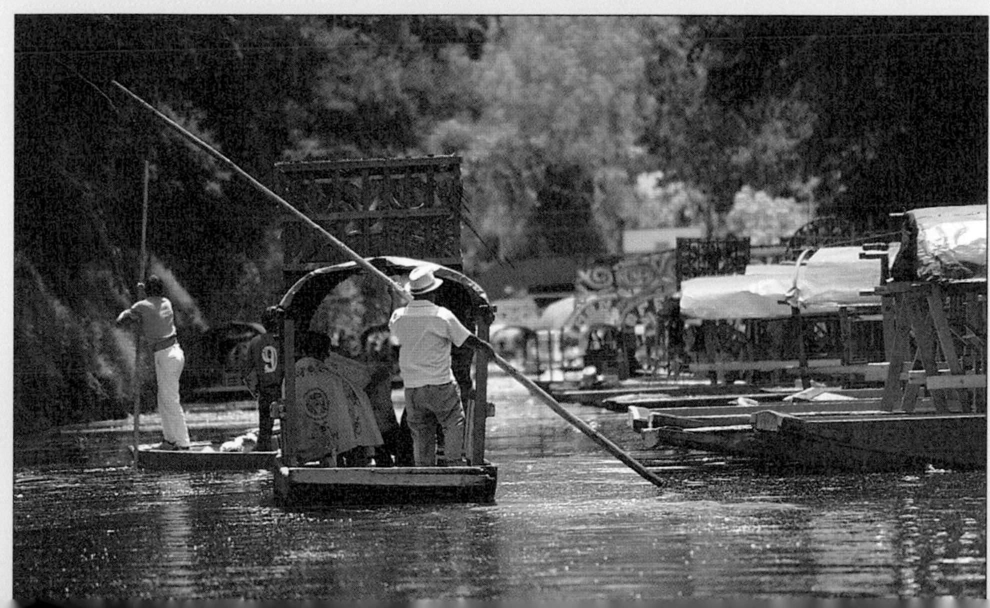

Text permissions

We wish to thank the authors, publishers, and holders of copyright for their permission to reprint the following:

Excerpts from *Sandra Cisneros: Writing About Her Heritage* from *U.S. Express*, February, 1991. Copyright © 1991 by Scholastic, Inc. Reprinted by permission of Random House.

The Harder They Come by James Chambers (Jimmy Cliff). Copyright © 1972 Reprinted by permission of Polygram Music Publishers, Inc.

Photo Credits

Unit 1

Chapter Opener

xx,1 © Richard Hutchings/Photo Researchers, Inc.

Text

3 Left to Right: © Susan Van Etten, © Shirley Zeiberg/Photo Reseachers, Inc.
4 Clockwise from top right: © Index Stock, © Rhoda Sidney/Monkmeyer Press, © Jeff Greenberg/The Picture Cube, © Steven Cohen/Index Stock
5 Clockwise from top left: © Index Stock, © Dennis McDonald/The Picture Cube, © Spencer Grant/The Picture Cube, © Stock Imagery
7 © Jeffrey Meyer/Stock Imagery
8 © Jeffrey Meyer/Stock Imagery
10 Clockwise from top left: © Robert Daemmrich/Tony Stone Worldwide Ltd.,© Larry Lawfer/The Picture Cube, © Robert Brenner/PhotoEdit, © Owen Franken/Stock Boston, © Brent Jones/Stock Boston
11 Clockwise from top right: © Stock Imagery, © Aneal Vohra/Unicorn Stock, © Stock Imagery, © Martin Jones/Unicorn Stock
12 Clockwise from bottom left: Stephen Frisch/Stock Boston, © Jim Zuckerman/Westlight, © Bob Daemmrich/The Image Works, © Spencer Grant/Monkmeyer Press
13 Clockwise from top left: © Jeffrey Meyers/Stock Imagery, © Jeff Greenberg/Unicorn Stock Photos, © Freeman/Grishaber/PhotoEdit
14 © Robert Brenner/PhotoEdit

Unit 2

Chapter Opener

16 Clockwise from top left: © Georgen Goodwin/Monkmeyer Press, © Michal Herron/Woodfin Camp and Assoc., © Comstock, Mimi Forsyth/Monkmeyer Press, © Rob Crandall/ Stock Boston, © Rick Kopstein/Monkmeyer Press
17 Clockwise from top left: Bob Daemmrich/Stock Boston, © Index Stock, © Jeff Greenberg/Photo Researchers, Inc., © R. Sydney/The Image Works

Text

18 Top to bottom: © Index Stock, © B. Daemmrich/The Image Works
19 Clockwise from top left: © Index Stock, © Index Stock, © The Picture Cube, © Sullivan/Index Stock
21 Clockwise from top left: © Richard Hutchings/Photo Researchers Inc., © Jeff Greenberg/Photo Researcher Inc., © Bob Daemmrich/Stock Boston, © Index Stock, © Peter Vandermark/Stock Boston
23 Clockwise from top left: © Arthur Tilley/FPG Int'l., Eric Kopstein/Monkmeyer Press, © Ellis Herwig/The Picture Cube, © Rhoda Sidney/The Image Works
25 © Index Stock
26 Clockwise from top left: © Mike and Carol Werner/Comstock, © Bruce Ando/Index Stock, © Stock Imagery, © Mike and Carol Werner, Comstock
28 Clockwise from top left: Edward Keating, Peter Britton, Peter Britton, Peter Britton
29 Left to right: © Comstock, © Comstock
31 © Comstock
35 © James Lemass/The Picture Cube

Unit 3

Chapter Opener

36 3PO

Text

51 © Comstock
54 Clockwise from top left: The Smithsonian Institution, Nation Museum of American History, National Numismatic Collection, © Stock Imagery, © Stock Imagery, © Stock Imagery, From the World Book Encyclopedia. © 1993 World Book Inc., By permission of the publisher, From the World Book Encyclopedia. © 1993 World Book Inc., By permission of the publisher

55 Clockwise from top left: © Aneal Vohra/The Picture Cube, © Peter L. Chapman, © Peter L. Chapman, © Peter Menze/Stock Boston
56 Top to bottom: UPI/Bettmann, © By the White House Historical Association; Photographs by the National Geographic Society
57 Clockwise from top left: UPI/Bettman, UPI/Bettmann, By the White House Historical Association; Photographs by the National Geographic Society

Chapter 4

Text

72 Clockwise from top left: © Comstock, © Index Stock, © Fred Busk/Peter Arnold, Robert Capece/Monkmeyer Press, Leo deWys Inc., © Peter Arnold
73 © Index Stock
75 Clockwise from top left: © Comstock, © Comstock, © Index Stock, © Index Stock, © Index Stock, Leo deWys Inc.
76 Clockwise from top left: Tony Stone World Wide Ltd., © Susan Van Etten, © Index Stock, © Comstock

Chapter 5

Chapter Opener

82 Clockwise from top left: © Daemmrich/Stock Boston, Jeff Shultz/Leo deWys Inc., © Cary Wolinsky/Stock Imagery, © Stock Imagery, © Peter Menze/Stock Boston
83 Clockwise from top left: © Bill Foley/Woodfin Camp & Assoc., Inc., © Grant LeDuc/Monkmeyer Press, Martha Bates/Stock Boston

Text

84 Clockwise from top left: © G. Zimbel/Monkmeyer Press, © Eunice Harris/The Picture Cube, © Susan Van Etten
85 Clockwise from top left: © Omar Marcus/Tony Stone World Wide, Ltd., Ellis Herwig/Stock Boston, © Gary Irving/Tony Stone World Wide, Ltd.
87 Left to right: © Comstock, © Don Smetzer/Tony Stone World Wide, Ltd.

Chapter 6

Chapter Opener

106 Left to right: © Mark Drewelow/Stock Imagery, © Bob Bennett/Stock Imagery, © John D. Luke/Index Stock
107 Left to right: © Stock Imagery, © Michael J. Howell/Index Stock

Text

110 Left to right: © Comstock, © J. K. Lange/Stock Imagery
111 Top to bottom: © Tom Walker/Stock Imagery, © Comstock, © Gordon Wiltsie/APA/Black Star
112 Top left: © Will Steger/APA/Black Star, © Will Steger/APA/Black Star
120 Jay Dickman & Skeeter Hagler
123 David Muench
124 Clockwise top right: Tom Till, © Jim Markham
125 © Lawrence Migdale/Stock Boston

Chapter 7

Chapter Opener

126 Clockwise top left: © Index Stock, © Comstock, © Index Stock, © Index Stock
127 Top to bottom: © Index Stock, Rhoda Sidney/Leo deWys

Text

141 Left to right: Courtesy Crawford County Historical Society, Meadville, PA, © Peter L. Chapman
144 © Shel Silverstein

Chapter 8

Chapter Opener

148 Clockwise top left: Luis Castaneda/The Image Bank, © Milton Feinberg/Stock Boston, Rafael Macia/Photo Researchers, © Bob Daemmrich/The Image Works, © Stock Boston, © A. Reininger/Woodfin & Assoc., © Lee Waldman/Tony Stone World Wide, Ltd.
149 Clockwise top left: © Paul Conklin/Monkmeyer Press, © Lindsay Hebberd/Woodfin Camp & Assoc., © John Yurka/The Picture Cube

Text

151 © Richard Pasley/Stock Boston
152 © J. Sohm/The Image Works
153 © J. Sohm/The Image Works
158 Ruben Guzman
161 Cumpleanos, © Carmen Lomas Garza
169 Clockwise top right: © Susan Van Etten/The Picture Cube, © Bob Daemmrich/Stock Boston
165 Clockwise top right: © Susan Van Etten/The Picture Cube, © Susan Van Etten/The Picture Cube